T0161276

TONING

The Creative and Healing Power of the Voice

"Sound is the meeting place of the abstract and manifested idea."

— LAUREL ELIZABETH KEYES

"For the first two days of the New Year (1981), I sat in meditation with a hum in my breath. Then I listened to Bach, Mozart and Satya Sai Baba as I hummed. I moved, I did yoga, I toned. That week was the great transition for my inner life and profession. I knew that tone and music were healing agents for release and re-alignment. Both the art and joy of music became a force that spoke more to my soul than to my conscious mind. Now, nineteen books later and entering my sixth decade, I return to the power of tone, affirmations, and classical music as gateways to balance and health. Laurel Elizabeth Keyes' book is fundamental to this work."

— DON CAMPBELL

TONING

The Creative and Healing Power of the Voice

Laurel Elizabeth Keyes

New edition of the groundbreaking book
with additional insight by

Don Campbell

Best-selling author of *The Mozart Effect*

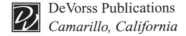
DeVorss Publications
Camarillo, California

ISBN: 9780875168319
Library of Congress Control Number: 2007920408
Third Printing, 2017

DeVorss & Company, Publisher
P.O. Box 1389
Camarillo CA 93011-1389
www.devorss.com

Printed in the United States of America

CONTENTS

Toning CD

* Permission granted by Sun-Scape Enterprises, Limited; Text © 1995,
  Kenneth George Mills; Music © 1995, Tim Janis. All rights reserved.
  The Kenneth G. Mills Foundation
  P.O. Box 790, Station F
  Toronto, Ontario, Canada M4Y 2N7

  Tel: 416-410-0453 or 1-800-437-1454
  www.kgmfoundation.org

FOREWORD

Opening the Doors of Tone
by Don Campbell

THE LIFE OF MUSIC around me took on an altogether new and perplexing dimension when I met Laurel Keyes in 1978. As a professional musician, journalist and teacher, music had always been a tool for emotional and artistic expression as well as endless hours of joyous entertainment. Being interested in the transformational and spiritual aspects of music, I was stunned when introduced to this small, radiant and energetic woman.

Before I met Laurel, while living in Japan, a book by Dorothy Retallack, *The Sound of Music and Plants,* was sent to me as a gift. Written as a project for a master's degree in music, she created a greenhouse experiment on the effect of different styles of music on the growth of plants. The little book was a fascinating observation on the effect of continuously played music on the growth rate and flowering rhythms of plants. Simply stated, loud and dissonant music retarded growth. The music of Bach as well as Indian ragas enhanced the rate of growth and the flowering of plants.

I began correspondence with Dorothy and she invited me to Denver in 1978 to meet "the most amazing woman who healed with tone." As I walked into the living room of a modest and comfortable Craftsman home, I met Laurel and her son Paul Chivington. The conversation was lighthearted and refreshing, but soon I realized that it was not music that fascinated her, it was the power of tone. She was interested in the "oneness of sound," that unornamented sonic power which was not embellished by rhythm, melody or harmony. She was clear that the power within a tone "restores people to their harmonious patterns."

As she stood in front of me and began to sound, I felt as if I was in front of a generator. My body responded to the power more potently than my ears heard the sound. She knew that the energy of the voice could be used to balance the spirit, the mind and the body. It was a type of internal tuning fork that brought alignment to life, dispelled pain and instilled some mystical type of spiritual perception.

What I was hearing was somehow primordial. It was the energy within sound. It was expressive, but not sentimental. It was raw, yet elegant. I sensed that within the tones that I felt and heard lived the fundamental core of sound. This energy was within all auditory vibration whether it be loud, soft, muted or energized.

My musically educated ears were forced to become dormant while I opened myself to another world of sound. It was more of a feeling, an energetic blast of kindness, sweetness and genuine well-being. Within a few seconds, my world of sound had changed. Being attuned to the melodies and harmonies of Western music, it was necessary to await the melody or harmonic progression to feel the effect of music. However, this new experience within a short moment of toning had both an immediate affect and effect.

Laurel gave me a copy of one of her books as well as a pamphlet she had written called, *Toning, The Lost Word.* I had felt this was an important meeting for me, something I could not quite understand, but profound in its physical and emotional impact. Over the coming months I began an improvisational regimen of sounding my voice without the primary concern for the "beauty of performance" as I was taught in music school. It was the beginning of the search for a simple form of becoming present, in the large "here and now" of sound.

The closest musical experience with tone I had to that point in my life was in my graduate school studies of Indian music. I knew the power of the drone, the elongated constant sounds that accompany the *ragas* or scales and melodies. Played as the repetitive and constant sound on the tambura, the drone serves as the groundwork for all the improvisations of the solo instrument, the sitar or vena. Yet the drone was not played alone for extended periods of time. Its bright and complex overtones created a harmonic textural canvas for melodies and rhythms to dance upon. The drone maintains the tone, the heart of the sound. The drone is like a sonic foundation upon which a musical structure is built. The tone now became for me the heart of every sound through which a rhythm flowed.

Returning to Dallas from meeting Laurel in Denver, I would remember to hum a little every day as I would meditate. I would randomly find a sound that felt right and just see what would happen in four or five minutes. I quickly discovered that when my jaw was relaxed and my eyes were closed, the sound flowed and I began to feel a unique and balancing quality. After three to five minutes of Toning, I would have a clear mind similar to that of a long meditation session. When I toned with energy, I was immediately refreshed. Something important was happening to me. I had found the wellspring of sound.

For the next three years, I experimented without any kind of organized routine. I worked as educational director of choral activities for a national organization and enjoyed my musical life, but felt that something was missing from weekly performing and listening activities. Then in 1979, my father died unexpectedly, my job became stressful and my doctor found a strange lump in the upper part of my left lung. He found some degeneration in my bones and insisted I was under too much stress. My doctor was killed suddenly in a car accident and I found myself unable to meditate, exercise or concentrate. For two years, I felt unfocused and at odds with my professional life.

On New Year's Eve in 1981, I wrote in my journal about the challenges of previous years. I sat alone with my rage, grief, frustration and fear and started to sob. From my groans and cries, a tone emerged from my gut. In a few minutes the sound thundered from my body as I climbed on my desk and the despair and pain in me sounded for nearly an hour. The long extended vocalizations moved from whispers to roars. I pounded a drum, I screamed survival and the tone continued for hours. The spectrum of these primitive and rich sounds was broad, the emotions were raw. These physical and mental releases were like the end of a long trance of pain and darkness. My inner life had been caged and it was breaking free through sounding.

For the first two days of the New Year, I sat in meditation with a hum in my breath. I napped with a sound in my heart and head. I felt gloriously empty, tender, quiet. Then I listened to Bach, Mozart and Satya Sai Baba as I hummed. I moved, I did yoga, I toned. Then, I slept for a full day as if I were on a boat in the ocean of sound.

That week was the great transition for my inner life and profession. I knew that tone and music were healing agents for release and realignment. Both the art and joy of music became a force that spoke more to my soul than to my conscious mind. I recalled how I heard and felt music as a child and suddenly could see how others could benefit from the fundamental power and vibration of sound.

I had been initiated into "tone." Laurel's words about tone "restoring people to their harmonious patterns" came to mind. I noticed how easy it was to relax, to meditate and to move. Within the ensuing months, my job dissolved and my health returned to normal with no signs of abnormality.

I began to listen to a quiet inner world, almost a tone, and sensed a new quality of perception and sensation within the body. I had moved through a portal that would change the direction of all my future work with music, education and health.

Now, nineteen books later and entering my sixth decade, I return to this power of tone. Last year I wrote *Creating Inner Harmony,* a book that utilizes tone, visualization, affirmations and classical music as gateways into balance and health. During the year of experimentation, I realized how important the work done by the mentors and students at the Institute for Music, Health and Education would be for the future. I wrote *The Roar of Silence* in 1989 and its success brought many students to the Institute in search of what makes tone so powerful and useful in health-care. During its nine years of outreach through correspondence classes, seminars, and workshops, over a thousand students began to explore the power of tone. Five hundred students took courses on health, color and vocal sounds, and nearly a hundred completed all the courses.

Laurel Keyes' book is fundamental to this work. In the following pages you will find her original writings. On the enclosed CD you will hear her speak about the powers of tone. After her text, I will explore the research from the Institute for Music, Health and Education and provide exercises that can assist the tonal journey in your own personal life.

My sincere thanks go to Barbara Dalberg, who has kept the interest in Laurel Keyes' work alive for the past twenty-five years and who has worked with me in creating this new edition. Appreciation goes to Gary Peattie, publisher of DeVorss & Co.; to Catherine Viel, my editor; to Bill Horwedel, my manager at Spring Hill Media in Boulder; and to Susan Alberghini and Ellen Mann at the Kenneth G. Mills Foundation for their assistance with the enclosed recording.

May you be inspired by the simplicity of this dynamic exploration into your voice, your sound and your soul.

> – Don Campbell
> *Boulder, Colorado, 2008*

"From the practical to the mystical, Toning has a place in each day. May you find joy in this simple way of being in harmony."

— DON CAMPBELL

Toning

PART I

PREFACE

by Laurel Elizabeth Keyes

A BOOK IS SUPPOSED TO HAVE A PREFACE, but it is my opinion that few people read prefaces. They hurry into the book to find if there is something that can be useful to them.

However, if you are one of those few who takes time to read this, let me assure you that the idea of Toning is not a theory that I am trying to prove. It is a result I have observed, and I have tried to report all the material in this book as factually as possible.

Toning is an ancient method of healing, which I hope will be recognized and used with new understanding now that we have more scientific explanations for it. It does not depend upon faith, nor belief in the method, any more than these are necessary to our use of electricity to provide light and energy in our daily living. There appear to be certain natural flows of energy in our bodies and if we recognize them and cooperate with them, they benefit us.

Is there a connection between Toning and glossolalia, or the speaking in tongues?

There may be an ancient tie, for glossolalia was practiced in the Eleusinian and other Mystery schools in both Western and Eastern cultures. Long before recorded history, "before the coming of churches and temples, before men were certain about the object of their worship, an inner awareness of something higher and greater than themselves filled their hearts with rapture and their tongues with praise."*

But as speaking in tongues is generally understood, it is a practice of Christians, dependent upon faith and considered to be a gift of the Holy Spirit.

Toning is not limited to one's religion, or lack of it. It does not require one's belief. Apparently it is not a "gift" but something available to anyone who goes through the mechanics of letting the voice express itself in a natural way. Anyone who can groan can Tone and experience its benefits.

The greatest difference is that the person who is Toning is watching the process and, after the first sigh, directs it consciously. The subjective surrender to some personality outside of one's self, acknowledged by the glossolalist, is absent. Toning is a very positive, consciously directed identification with the inner power of life, and the full awareness of the release of it at will. Rather than being submissive or losing consciousness, the

Toner is extremely alert and the feeling is one of new control—of one's self, one's world and affairs; a new awareness of the unity with all life and one's inherent divinity, waiting to be recognized and claimed.

There is no mystery about Toning. It can be understood through material science, physiology and psychology as well as the most ancient concepts of our relationship to God.

Please try it.

* Bach, Marcus, Ph.D., *The Inner Ecstasy*, Abingdon Press, Nashville, Tenn. 1969.

CHAPTER 1

Toning–What it Is

by Laurel Elizabeth Keyes

THE DISCOVERY of what we call *Toning* came about accidentally.

Most discoveries are only uncovering some ancient wisdom that has been buried in time and circumstances, but this discovery was accidental in that we did not start with a theory which we attempted to prove. Toning just happened. We watched it, and its beneficial results, then studied the influence of sound vibrations upon the body. From the result we worked back, like Newton with his apple, to the cause and the laws that brought it about.

We began with the idea that few people realize that their lives can be changed, that they have the power to control the life forces and reform their life patterns, through sound.

Consider the power we exert through ordinary speech. With words we can create images in another's mind similar to the ones held in our own.

Think, really think, what a miracle it is that a person who sees an object, such as a vase, can use sound in the form of words to cause an image of it to form in another's mind so clearly that the object could be identified among many objects. Even more, consider the miracle that enables a person to transmit a non-objective, abstract thought to another's mind. Or, stretching our small perceptions to comprehend something of the speed of light, then imagining stars, millions of light years away from our small planet. No other creatures can do that, and it is based on sound.

We create with words and sound. Almost all our actions and reactions result from words. It is generally accepted that we cannot think without words or symbols, and that our thinking is limited to them. Words are tools. It is important to have a good selection at our command.

Beneath these words are the vibrations of the tone upon which they travel. Tone is the underlying force operating in our lives. To understand this enhances our ability to create what we wish and to give form and substance to the ideas in our minds. Sound is the meeting place of the abstract and manifested idea.

This practice of Toning began for me one day after a study group had gone and I was standing alone in the room, enjoying the stillness and the charged atmosphere which remains after such a meeting. I noticed a sensation in my chest and throat as though a force were rising, wanting to be released in sound, but then it would subside again. It was the feeling that might cause one to burst into song—for no known reason—or to gasp as one might when coming upon a beautiful scene. I observed this as it rose and subsided, almost a thing apart because certainly I was doing nothing to cause this. It had a volition of its own and an apparent desire to express. It was an odd experience to both watch it and feel it, without making any effort to direct it or control it. I watched with curiosity.

I found my lips parting and my mouth opened very slightly in an easy relaxed manner so that the teeth were just barely parted. Unexpectedly a sound bubbled up, like something tossed up on a fountain spray. A single syllable emerged—"Ra."

I couldn't have been more astonished. I did not use Egyptian terms and we had not been discussing that culture. Why the sound took that form was as bewildering to me as if some other foreign language might have sprung from my throat. It came up again, paused as though frightened, but when it was not stopped it came out and soared.

To describe it I would liken it to a bird that had been caged all its life and found the door of its cage opened. It tried its wings, scarcely knowing what to expect, and finding it could be lifted in flight, it flew in delighted abandonment.

The feeling was as though these sounds came from the earth itself, and poured up through a silver tube, through my throat, effortlessly, freely as artesian water flows from the ground. I did not take a deep breath, as a singer, but the note was sustained as though supplied by a limitless source, and it went into heights that I couldn't have reached normally since my voice is rather low.

I decided that I must be in some phase of meditative state so I would tape the sound and evaluate it in a more rational mood. I did. The next day, when I listened to the recording, I was still amazed. This was not "my" voice. Yet it was not someone else's as in the case of trance medium demonstrations. It belonged to my body, but I had never been able to use it in this manner before. Perhaps that explained it. I had not used it. It had been free of my mind's domination and had expressed itself.

I concluded that since most animals have a voice—birds sing, dogs bark, cows moo, cats purr, and so forth—it is our physical body that has a voice. *It is dominated by intellectual direction and it is allowed to express only as the mind dictates.*

This creative force, which does not belong to the mind, is enslaved by the mind, and is therefore rebellious. Only in a groan, scream, or sigh, and in laughter, does it come out unhindered by the mind. One does not *think* a groan. It bursts through the mental restrictions and with it certain tensions are released. Many women say that groaning during childbirth is a great help. Animals in pain groan. Pain frequently is the result of tension, and groaning is nature's way of relieving it.

Infants have a language of Toning. Their little cries and murmurings express body feelings. People remark, "The baby is singing himself to sleep." Funny little grunts and sounds that must be pleasing to him. As soon as the baby learns to combine mental images with the voice, the natural sounding is curtailed and interference is imposed upon the body-voice. This begins to close the door between the conscious and subconscious mind; between thinking and feeling communication.

As I continued to experiment with this body-voice I realized that there was much more to it than just a release of tension. Each time that I Toned, my body felt exhilarated, *alive* as it had never felt before, with a feeling of wholeness and extreme well-being.

I became curious about the source of this energy. Knowing a woman who had properly diagnosed ulcers, tumors, and other ailments with her "X-ray vision," I asked her to watch this body-voice in expression.

She said that the Tone was a force she saw as swirling movement in the area of the reproductive organs, which then appeared to draw magnetic currents up from the earth through the feet and limbs and rose in a spiral of light to the throat area.

When I let it pass out, freely, with no attempt to control it, it appeared to cleanse the entire body, releasing tensions and congested areas. She said that the body, afterwards, had an appearance of balance, like an engine that has been overhauled and all parts are working together with precision, or a harp which has been tuned and the slack strings tightened, and the taut ones eased to make a harmonious whole.

She noticed that when I decided to direct the Tone, the force collapsed back into the pelvic region, or into the solar plexus where it tightened into feelings I might interpret as frustration, anxiety, annoyance.

I was convinced that there had to be a relationship between this natural body-voice and the mind without conflict, and with benefit to both. Psychologists have agreed that most of our problems arise from the subconscious, the feeling nature. "When the mind and the feelings are in conflict, the feelings usually win."

Anyone who has tried to diet, stop smoking or overcome some habit knows that to think about doing it, even deciding to do it, does not assure the cooperation of the necessary willpower. This has been one of the mysteries of human functioning. Even St. Paul complained, "For the will is present with me; but *how* to perform that which is good I find not. For the good that I would I do not; but the evil which I would not, that I do."[1]

Apparently the will is held by unconscious feelings, and until we can find a way to release it from that hold, to be directed by the mind, we live divided and frustrated lives.

So began the exciting search. I felt that in Toning I had been given a key to unlock this storehouse of the will.

Take a Moment

- Before you read the next chapter, close your eyes and observe your breath.

- Notice the rhythm of each inhalation and exhalation.

- Let your mind reflect on what you have read and experience the calming presence of your breath.

"Everyone who wills can hear the inner voice. It is within everyone."

— MOHANDAS GANDHI

CHAPTER 2

Search in Myth, Legend, Religions

by Laurel Elizabeth Keyes

FOLLOWING THE SOUND-IDEA as a thread back through other cultures—Grecian, Chinese, Persian, Indian, Native American and primitive peoples—I found that it was related to the oldest methods of healing. Two things were common in most healing rituals: sound or chanting, and rhythmic movements, either in dance or stomping.

Sound vibrations appeared to be associated with creation, whether it was of the world or our individual life patterns. "In the beginning was the Word—" Word has been translated in various ways from *Logos*, as law, archetypal pattern, and so forth. Philo wrote that "His image is THE WORD, a form more brilliant than fire; the Logos is the vehicle by which God acts on the universe, and may be compared to the speech of man."[2] These translations emphasized *vibration*, not word.

I began weaving these threads from ancient philosophical teachings and religious concepts into a pattern. I found that Chinese healers had used "singing stones" in their rituals. These were thin, flat plates of jade which, when struck, gave off musical tones. They had designated the Great Tone of Nature, *Kung,* which seems to correspond to our musical note of F. The Sufis considered *Hu* to be the creative sound. The Tibetans considered the notes of A, F sharp and G to be powerful sacred sounds. We are familiar with the importance given the words *Aum* and *Amen.* Amen was more than a period to a prayer when it was first uttered. It was derived from the older "Aum" which represented all of the sounds which the human voice was capable of expressing and therefore associated with the creative principle designating God.

Pythagoras taught that sound was a creative force and that music held therapeutic benefits to the body. The Mystery Schools following these teachings associated *rhythm* with the body and *melody* with the emotions; *harmony* lifted consciousness to spiritual awareness. This concept did not originate with Pythagoras, of course. It was used by civilizations in the remote past and he carried it on.

Along with references to sound, I found the traditional story of the Fall of Man in all of the religious teachings and Mystery initiations. The statement that "Matter is condensed energy," attributed to Einstein, was given in older terms as "Man is condensed, or lowered, spirit." There was a definite correlation between the vibrations of spirit and the physical human body.

The word "man" coming from the Sanskrit root "manus" (thinking creature) indicated that the fall of man meant the fall of consciousness into a lower state of functioning.

One of the most common ancient beliefs, expressed in philosophies and religions, is that the soul, or individualized portion of God, was attracted to sensations and experiences to be found in the animal nature and became trapped there. It formed an identity with the animal nature and forgot its true origin and power. The Egyptians taught that the body was a prison for the soul but the latter was not condemned to eternal banishment and imprisonment. The Father of the World permits its chains to be broken, and has provided in the course of Nature the means of its escape.

All scriptural teachings are based upon the struggle of this divine part of the human to free itself from animality and return to its rightful heritage: the effort to bring the thinking and feeling qualities into accord with the harmonic pattern in which the human was created, "in the image of God."

The rational mind was considered to be an extension of the soul, or the buffer zone, between the two natures, for if the soul knowing no danger or pain had directed the physical body without recognition of the laws governing flesh and bone, it would have destroyed the vehicle.

If the urges of the physical body were not balanced by the wisdom of the soul, people would become selfish and cruel. It would be easy to lose all of the finer human urges, urges which result in expressions of love, honor, and aspiration. Art and music, fine architecture and law, science and healing—none of humanity's highest achievements would have come into being.

In the Edenic story we find this theme. Until humans developed minds capable of choosing (eating of the "fruit of the tree of knowledge of good and evil") we lived in peace. When the mind developed and began taking the consciousness into areas of sense perception, tasting, seeing, desiring, we were cut off from our effortless existence and sent out on the long journey to find our inherent divinity again through experiencing free will and choice. These choices would bring us, eventually, either to identify with our true nature, or to suffer the "eternal" separation.

An American Indian legend, from the Hopis, tells of creation of the First People. The Spider Woman molded the earth, mixed with her saliva, into forms in the image of the Universal God, Sotuknang. When she uncovered them, the forms came to life. But they could not speak. Since Spider Woman received her power from Sotuknang, she had to appeal to Him to give them voice. "Also the wisdom and power to reproduce, so that they may enjoy their life and give thanks to the Creator."[3] Sotuknang granted this wish so the forms could speak and reproduce. (There appears to be a linking of the idea of creative productivity—the voice and sex organs. This may relate to the phenomenon of the voice change in the male at puberty.) These First People had no illness because they were of "One Heart." But when some permitted evil *feelings* to enter, they were said to have Two Hearts and then began the troubles. So the legends, myths and scriptures portrayed the human state.

How could these opposite aspects of a person be brought back together—soul, mind and body, functioning in harmony?

Through "The Word." Chants, mantras and prayers held a prominent place in achieving this union, for they followed the natural pattern of creation and exercised will.

Two recurring ideas dominated the ancient teachings. The first was that a Father-Mother union of spirit and matter (or positive and negative forces) resulted in the creation of humanity as well as all things. The second idea was that Will motivated human beings. How we came to be and how we lived, in peace or in conflict, was a result of the application of Will.

It became apparent that the voice is a vehicle which the mind uses for its manifestations. *It is the womb impregnated with the seed of the idea.* It is the higher creative force as the reproductive organs of the body are the lower.

35

It is not necessary to go into great detail in supplying references since you are not reading this book to become a scholar but to be able to use your own voice in a beneficial manner. But I would like to mention a few intimations of the Spirit-breath-sound, and matter-form relationship from varying sources.

Brahm is said to have "breathed out and creation was formed. *Brahm* breathed in and took the creation back into Himself."

Plato said, "The Word is number manifested by form."[4] We have St. John's "In the beginning was the Word." From the Hebrews there is Genesis 2:7, "And the Lord God formed man of the dust of the ground and breathed into his nostrils the breath of life; and man became a living soul." The Egyptians taught that the Father or the Spirit was the *generative* power; the Mother, or form, was the *conceptive* power; the issue or product of this union was the Child.

In other words, "everything that is" results from a union of positively and negatively charged units of energy. The negative force, or mother, is that which is acted upon. In the human, it becomes the *feelings* which give form to the *idea*. But whether the substance which takes the idea is for a statue or a garment, or is the steel and concrete giving form to a picture in the architect's mind, or is used for healing the body, the manifestation is from the surrender of negative force to positive. The negative aspect must yield and permit itself to be used, and then molds its properties into the form of the positive pattern.

There can be no harvest without seed in the soil, no child without the union of man with woman, no anything without this combination of positive and negative forces. And, it must be remembered that it is the mother which gives birth, not the father. *Feeling must be fecundated by idea or image to bring about results.*

This may explain why many prayers, affirmations and positive thinking seem to fail. They remain solitary. The idea has no mate to give birth to the desired offspring—mental pictures which have not stirred feelings into productivity.

Too often the mind dominates the voice ruthlessly, so it encounters resistance. It behaves as a rapist of the body forces, using them without consideration. *Feeling* then rejects the *idea.*

The feeling-voice should be wooed lovingly. When it is permitted its own expression, as in Toning, it feels secure and protected. It surrenders and receives the idea given it by the mind and, eager to be a part of creation, it gives birth to that form. It is joyous cooperation rather than rebellious slavery.

The conclusion which may be drawn from these old concepts is that Spirit is consciousness. It has collected around Itself a shape, or body, through which to contact experience on this more dense plane of vibration, and to raise it, transform it into Itself, through "the Word."

Take a Moment

- Observe your breath. Has it changed since the end of the last chapter? Consider the formation of words when you speak. Are they at the beginning or the end of an exhalation?

- Use the word "Peace" and observe where sound begins in your breath. "In the beginning was the Word." Where is the beginning of the word in your breath?

"All objects have a spiritual tone at the foundation of their being, and, in this deepest nature, man himself is such a spiritual tone."

— RUDOLPH STEINER

CHAPTER 3

Voice Creates Life Patterns

by Laurel Elizabeth Keyes

COUNT ALFRED KORZYBSKI, father of General Semantics, referred to the cortex as a corn which had formed over the thalamic stem from the irritation and pressures of civilization.

In the last century we have let these pressures drive us more into our mental interests and farther away from our natural body expressions. We ride more and walk less. We sit more and stand less. We eat more and digest less. It might be said, also, that "we speak more and say less." We have grown farther away from communication with our inner nature and its needs. We cannot repress a natural creative urge without seeing evidence of the distortion.

In not too distant times people gave voice to the sounds of their body language. People sang or whistled as they worked. Stories come to us of boatmen singing as they rowed, railroad workers pounding rails to ties with accompanying rhythms or song. Mothers hummed as they worked— usually nameless little songs that reflected their emotions; songs stirring with the whir of a spinning wheel, the thumping of a butter churn, or the hum of a sewing machine. Since woman first cradled her baby in her arms she has let her heart express in tender murmurings to heal a hurt or dispel a fear.

Folk songs and spirituals were born in this way. Even at the beginning of the twentieth century it was a common thing for family and friends to gather around the piano in the evening and sing. While these songs were patterned, they afforded the opportunity of self-expression for each person. They sang softly or loudly, took pride in their singing or made an effort to improve it. In this outlet there was a therapeutic process taking place, one which is sadly lacking now in the person who sits in a chair silently listening. Many people went to church more for the opportunity to sing out loudly in the sociability it afforded than for the sermon. Now there are choirs paid to sing, and while it may sound better to the listener, each body denied the joyful soaring of its own voice is suffering.

This may be one of the clues to the increase in neurosis and psychosomatic illness. Certainly there is growing evidence that noise and discordant sound (as in some of the so-called music) supplanting the natural voice expressions is in part to blame.

Dorothy Retallack did an interesting study on the effect of

sound on plant life. She had been intrigued by the reference to this in the first edition of this book and did the experiments at Colorado Women's College in Denver.[5]

In one of the most revealing of these experiments, the plants were subjected to a radio station which broadcast rock, and another which programmed classical and religious music. The plants leaned away from the rock broadcasting, some at 80-degree angles. Their root structures were shallow and these, too, grew away from the sound. Petunias refused to bloom. In contrast, squash vines wrapped themselves around the radio playing harmonious and religious music and there were six lovely blossoms on the petunia plant. Roots of these plants were plentiful and strong, the plants luxuriant in growth.

Her further studies on the response of plant life to sound caused her to comment, "I just can't help thinking that there is some combination of harmonic sounds that would improve human growth and heal illness."

Seeing plants react in this manner to sound causes us to wonder how much irreparable damage is being done to the human structure with civilization's increasing noise levels. It would seem that of all the pollutions about which we show concern, sound pollution could be the most dangerous. Yet it is something each of us can help to control, in our own lives, by the manner in which we use our voices.

By releasing tensions and stimulating circulation and nerve energy in the body, Toning is a natural method of healing. It releases the pattern of perfection within each person. Wonderful as are healing helps such as medicine, surgery, and so on, they are limited by the patient's ability to accept them. Unless there is full cooperation with the subconscious mind, the desired healing will not be lasting.

Physicians often are baffled when a patient has been cured of ulcers or some ailment and returns later with tumors, migraines or some other disorder. The patient's body was not in harmony with the pattern in his or her field. Surgery or medicine cannot eliminate hatred, fear or other feelings which cause deep-rooted problems. Seldom can talking about them (using the mind's concepts and symbols) result in changing the feelings; yet joyous feeling is so necessary for permanent correction.

Dr. William Tiller, a Guggenheim Fellow who worked with the Department of Materials Science at Stanford University, brought new light to this old problem when he stated, "All illness has its origin in a disharmony between the mind and spirit levels of the entity and that of the universal pattern for the entity. Thus, healing at the physical or even the etheric level is only temporary if the basic pattern at the mind and spirit level remains unchanged."[6]

Most of us have watched cobwebs form when dust particles

collect in a pattern made by air currents from a furnace or window, and while this is not an esthetic referent, it seems to me that as Tone goes out, it collects substance from the world around it, forming a very tangible manifestation.

When fine sand or sugar is sprinkled on a drumhead and put in contact with the vibrations coming from a violin or piano, the granules take on various geometric patterns; again we have evidence that sound can move matter, that vibrations can cause changes in the molecular structures.

The tone of a person's voice is highly indicative of his or her state, not only of health but of affairs. If the person's voice is whiny and has a sucking in or gasping sound, the person has a negative health condition. That quality of voice is often so discouraged or hopeless that self-pity becomes the positive polarity (instead of health), and no healing can be effected until the person reverses the tonal pattern. They are like a bottomless pit that will absorb all the help and attention provided, but will not use it to help themselves. They seem to cling to the problem or illness since that is what garners attention and importance! Their affairs are as sick as they are. They draw in negative conditions as a magnet attracts iron.

One can almost see the force of the voice of such a person spiraling counter-clockwise and down, rather than clockwise and up, which is a condition of health.

Then there is the tone which is thrust out but covers hostility, resentment and other negative conditions so that the person is always in trouble, in conflict, and "fighting for everything," and is generally disliked and unhappy. This type of person never asks a question—they demand an answer; and seldom get a satisfactory one because they frighten the person asked and cause so much confusion and chaos that inefficiency flourishes around them. Unfortunately this type of person is often in a position of authority (due to their forcefulness) and just by the tone of voice breeds hate and rebellion all around. They are accident-prone and trouble-saturated. In illness they suffer heart attacks, strokes, broken bones, falls and violent accidents; their tone attracts what they are—violence.

Conversely, the sucking-in, whining tone attracts lingering illness: cancer, asthma, allergies, tumors, rheumatism, arthritis, and so forth.

By the manner in which we speak, every hour of our lives, we set the pattern for our lives. When we realize the vastness of this power, we can appreciate the admonition in the Bible that we shall be held accountable for our every word.

Frequently I have watched amazing results come about in illness by just causing the person to change the tone in speaking. Instead of a sucking-in sound, to *thrust* the words out with vigor. By using his or her own voice to do this, an individual seems to change the polarity of their "field" and a healthy condition results.

One notable example was a woman who was suffering from mononucleosis and had been sent home, in her own conviction, "to die." She was in bed, of course, and so weak that it was difficult for her to speak over the telephone. I explained the Toning idea to her and asked her to work with me repeating simple words such as "I am going to get out of bed and do things that I want to do," but in a thrusting, positive way. (Even the word "thrust" causes vigor. The *th* sound is one of positive push. One could hardly draw in one's last dying breath with a good "th" sound.)

"Give it more THRUST," I encouraged her, and finally, with some indignation, she responded, "I *am* thrusting my words out." From that moment on it seemed the force was reversed from negative to positive polarity. The next day she was not only out of bed, but was doing some work, and on the third day she drove to a nearby town to hear a lecture. There was no return of the illness. That day of changing her voice pattern began the change of her health.

It is not enough to let the negative feelings be released and expressed. Feelings of purpose must replace them—the person must be inspired to feel that they are noble, good and worthy because that is their true state—the pattern of perfection in their field.

"What gets your attention gets you." When one dwells upon weaknesses and faults one pours more energy into them and they seem to grow—talking about them, giving new birth to them so that in turn there are more troubles to talk about. It becomes a vicious circle.

Some people insist that they would be hypocrites to say they feel good or happy when they feel inferior and miserable. They want to be "themselves." But, what self? Why identify with one's lowest nature? Why not identify with the inherent perfect pattern in the field as Dr. Tiller described it? That is the real Self.

"Be ye perfect, even as your father in heaven is perfect" is not a pretty but impossible dream. It is a direction, a statement of fact. We are fashioned "in the image of God" (perfection). Until we reinstate ourselves in it, become one with that pattern, sorrows and problems are the natural results of separation.

When illness or misfortune comes into a life, a person often cries, "Why should this happen to me? Why does God punish me so?"

To ask that is about as sensible as to step off a ten-story building and, finding oneself crushed on the ground, ask, "Why does the ground punish me so?"

We should ask, "What have I done to separate me from my right pattern of health? What lesson am I to learn from this?" If electrical current does not flow into an appliance it is not that it is trying to punish it—it is probable that a fuse has been blown by overuse, or the appliance has broken down from neglect. Let us find the cause and correct it. Refuse to suffer for nothing! Learn from it and get your value's worth from the payment.

We do not live in a world common to all people. We live in our private little cocoon worlds which we create from our thoughts and feelings—our memories, desires, reactions and evaluations. *These are the substances which form upon the forces of life,* as cobwebs form upon currents of air, according to our conscious or unconscious direction. "We make our habitation, as the worm spins silk, and dwell therein."

As an analogy, picture a girl taking a puppy on a leash for a walk. For the puppy's protection the leash is held in the girl's hand. Without it the puppy might dash out in front of a car, fall into some other danger, or be lost. If the puppy decides to rush headlong after a cat, he comes to the end of the leash and crashes to a painful halt. He gets up, looks at the girl, and must wonder, "How can she hurt me so if she loves me?"

When the dog learns obedience to its master's commands, the leash is removed. It is no longer necessary for the dog's safety.

When we dash off on our own desires, too often unwisely, we come to "the end of our rope," and are jerked up. The severity of the upsetting tumble depends upon the speed we are going in our independent pursuit. It is not the Master's wish to hurt us, but to save us from complete destruction that a rope is placed around us.

Through Toning, the body has the opportunity to slip into, and rest in our perfect pattern. It surrenders to the highest which the soul can direct the mind to imagine. In this people find peace and the answers to problems. Our heritage of joy and well-being is claimed.

Take a Moment

- Consider the ideas within this chapter. Begin to "hum" in a comfortable soft tone as you reflect on the powers of Tone.

"If you surrender completely to the moments as they pass, you live more richly those moments."

— ANNE MORROW LINDBERGH

CHAPTER 4

How to Tone

by Laurel Elizabeth Keyes

ONE OF THE BENEFITS to healing which Toning provides is cleansing of the field. Another is to invite the subconscious mind to cooperate with ideas held in the rational mind and to bring about a condition of wholeness—body, mind and soul.

Stand erect, with feet several inches apart. Stretch both arms high and let them drop back, shoulders swinging on the spine as a cross bar rests on top of a T, in perfect balance.

The eyes must be closed. Begin to look inward, and *feel*.

Let the torso ride on the pelvic region and imagine the hipbones as protruding level auto headlights. (This is to counteract our usual tendency to cave in and bend forward.) Standing erect should cause no strain but give an easy, relaxed feeling. Let the body sway like a flower on its stalk in a breeze.

It is natural for all living things to move. The tides move, sap rises and falls in trees, plants move. It is unnatural for the body to be held in a rigid position. Let it sway slightly to get the feeling of the pulsation of life within it: the heartbeat, the flow of blood, the rhythm of breathing—finally, the oneness with all life throbbing in all of nature.

Feeling this magical process of aliveness within and around you, *let your body speak.* Relax the jaws so that the teeth are slightly parted. Let sound come up from it, not down upon it from the mind, but up from your feet. Let the body groan. It may be only an audible deep sigh but it is a feeling of release, of emptying out, of resting. Encourage it to be vocal. Always start with low groans.

Let the body groan as long as it likes and with abandon. You may think that you have nothing to groan about, but you will be surprised. All the hurts, physical and emotional, which you have received are buried in your subconscious memory, and groaning offers a release for them. Once the door is opened, repressed feelings of your entire life may begin to flow out. The groan may burst into protests such as "I'm tired of everything, my work, my family, of living, of struggling. I want freedom." Or, the voice may soar off into bird-like singing or spontaneous outpourings of worship or prayer. (For these reasons, Toning should be practiced alone whenever possible. At least the first few times.)

Whatever happens, do not let the mind influence it. Make the mind obedient, be still. Let it observe as it would a stage play where it would not presume to get into the act. Watch, and learn something of the host of this body house in which you, as consciousness, are only a guest.

Even in the first Toning session you will find that the voice, after groaning, is inclined to rise, siren-like, drop back and rise again, over and over until it reaches higher notes without effort.

The session may last ten minutes or an hour, but when the body feels cleansed *a sigh is released* and you know that the body-voice is satisfied. The involuntary sigh is the signal. You feel good. As though something had been accomplished, and you had brought yourself together into a harmonious whole. Confidence permeates you.

As you read this, notice how many times the word "let" is used. This is the most important factor of Toning. Let the body be free, let the voice be free, let health emerge. Don't strive, or impose direction upon the voice. You are going to learn to unfold from the inside out.

Toning stimulates the energy flowing in the body, causing a healthy glow. Even the medical phrase "body tone" indicates unconscious awareness of this. (How often we speak better than we know.) It releases the "Imprisoned Splendor" by bringing the mind and body together so that the inherent perfection of the field can manifest in both cell structure and ideal without interference or tensions.

As soon as the sigh is released and cleansing for that time is complete, something must be offered to fill the emptied cup. If possible, sit down for a few moments and enjoy the sense of peace. Let yourself enjoy the feeling of new aliveness, inside. You may wish to follow Toning with a meditation period, or sing a happy song. Whatever you do afterwards, you will be aware that you have "fastened the light" in yourself for the day.

You may object that there is no time for this. Is there time to be ill, unhappy, rushed or scattered? There is always time if we wish to do a thing.

For the busy, harassed parent, great benefits will be noticed by arising a half hour before the children in the morning and Toning softly where it will not disturb the household. It is a delightful feeling that one enjoys—a feeling of being ahead, instead of being rushed to keep up—to feel perfectly in control of oneself and the day and whatever it may bring. Tell your subconscious mind that "Some lovely thing is going to happen today," and it will begin to look for it, and bring it about.

Toning should be done upon first awaking or in the shower. Later in the day is better than not at all, but early morning helps you pull yourself together and set the pattern for the day.

While each individual's Toning pattern is different, as is a thumb print, you may feel that you have really found it when it follows this general pattern.

First phase: Relaxing the body in standing position, if possible. It can be done sitting in a car or in a chair, or even while lying in bed if one is ill, but let the body express itself in sound. Groan and watch the sound rise. The feeling is that an offering is being made. The life force within is eager to rise and be free.

Second phase: After the first few very low groans it will rise. Do not force it. Let it go where it wishes, until it rises to what it feels is a smooth high and flawless note. (Any strain defeats the purpose. Toning is release. Strain is imposed by the mind.)

It may be a new experience for you to feel an effortless action taking place in your body, yet this is the secret of good health, good emotional balance and clear thinking—to flow with life instead of fighting it.

Notice how your voice seems to long to rise into freedom. Let your mind witness this feeling and *expect your voice to rise* with the sense of joyous release that a child feels in throwing a ball to the sky.

Finally the body will be satisfied with what it feels is a perfect tone. This is the jewel which it offers in reverence to life. There will be a deep, contented sigh following that note. It is the signal that there is peace in your nature and your subconscious mind is ready to serve you. This ends the cleansing stage. Enjoy the feeling of being put together, as though you were wrapped in an impenetrable armor and filled with love for the whole world.

Now you are ready to accomplish something—to create with your voice, to Tone for others or some desired condition in your own life.

One may use the notes, A, B, C, and so on, as described in more detail later on. The vowel sounds can be used as vessels into which the Tone is poured and carried upwards. A-O-U-eeeeee.

Beginning with the "Ah" sound, watch the natural progression. Be aware of the tongue and mouth in the formation of the sounds.

"Ah" lets the tongue lie in a relaxed manner. "Oh" begins to draw the lip muscles into form and tightens control on the tongue. The "U" or oo-sound, as in *muse,* further controls the lips and raises the tongue. In the "E" sound, the tongue and breath are raised and all of the sound seems lifted from the throat to the head and there is a union of forces there.

The "E" sound is very powerful, especially if one consciously causes it to resonate in the upper part of the head. It should not be done too strenuously or long in the beginning. Find your own comfortable way, your own rhythm, through experience. Tone until you feel good, newly alive, enthusiastic.

It should cause one to feel that one is pilot of one's own craft, in complete command, flying above any difficulties and using even adverse winds to carry one to the desired destination.

Once you have found the benefit of Toning you will not give it up or let anything prevent your doing it. You will look back on your pre-Toning days as being only half alive, half a person. As one woman said, "I may forget to put my shoes on, or eat breakfast or a lot of things, but I wouldn't think of trying to face my day without Toning."

One may have felt depressed, ill, exhausted—it doesn't matter. From the first sound of Toning one notices a difference—it is taking *control* of one's body and life and, regardless of the negative condition, within a few minutes an improvement will be noticed. Toning shatters the negative condition. It is plugging into a power station and being recharged. It is using your willpower.

It is the voice which releases the power in the body, starts the motor *running* so the driver (the mind) may direct the car to where one wishes to go.

Your day isn't alive until you have begun its creation with "the Word."

It has been suggested that if one Toned, resonating the sound in a particular part of the brain which controlled an affected area of the body, correction might be made through that means. (This would amount to a sonar-acupuncture in the brain?) It sounds reasonable. Yogis have controlled their bodies for centuries with their science of brain and breath control. We know that a touch of a probe upon the brain will cause certain parts of the body to twitch; certain memories may be recalled. There is so much yet to be learned about the brain. Here might be an exciting frontier to explore, through sound.

When one has a pain somewhere in the body one begins Toning as low as the voice can reach, and slowly raises the pitch, as a siren sound rises. One will find that *there is a Tone which resonates with the pain and relieves the tension.* This is all done with sensitivity to feeling. To get an idea of this, place your finger against your nose and hum, directing the sound to that spot. Notice the sensation, inside, of the resonance. While this is not as definite in other parts of the body, it can be determined, and that is the tone that will relieve pain. Every pain has its companion Tone and by pulsating the Tone softly for a time—as long as it feels good, fifteen minutes or an hour—the pain will be relieved or eliminated. It is an escape valve for the pain because it is breaking up the tension which we label "pain" and it brings new life energy to that place. It is an inner sonar massage.

Many times, in a public lecture, I have asked someone in the audience who has a pain to come up and let this technique be demonstrated. As I stand facing the person, eyes closed and concentrating on the feeling of the sound, I start Toning very low and slowly, letting the sound scan the body. When the sound returns to me from the afflicted area I know it. It is an indescribable sensation: sticky and thick. There is no proper word but it is noticeable to me. I ask the person if that sound would seem more comfortable a little higher or lower—"This is the feeling that you have an inner itch and I am trying to let the sound scratch it—lower or higher?" This helps the person concentrate upon the exact area of distress. Then I pulsate the sound in a rhythmic manner, until my body sighs. Then I reach a high note with the feeling of energizing their own source of energy and let the sound sweep down through the body, perhaps two or three times.

The delightful thing is to witness their surprise when I open my eyes. "It's gone!" they exclaim in total unbelief. But it is gone, or at least helped. And I assure them that this is what they can do for themselves.

The problem may not always lie in the area of the pain. One interesting demonstration was that of a man who volunteered to have his headache relieved. He had been suffering with increasing and intensifying headaches. I started Toning at his feet and as the sound moved up I traced it up the inside of his leg, around the hip to his back, up the back to his neck, and finally to his head. But I could not hold the sound in his head area because it couldn't get past the "sticky" place in his foot.

"I'm sorry," I told him. "But the trouble seems to lie in your left foot."

"Nothing is wrong with my feet," he insisted.

The Tone wouldn't move up.

"Would you please sit down and press the inside of your arch? This is something which is puzzling me very much."

He sat down. He was wearing flat, hard-soled barefoot sandals. He began probing the area of the arch and he let out a yell, "Wow, that IS sore. I didn't know."

He was a heavy man and wearing that type of sandal gave no support to his arch.

"Maybe I should start wearing shoes," he decided.

Having found the source of the pain, we worked with sound all the way up and he found that the headache was eased and in a short time was gone.

When I demonstrate this technique it is in no manner intended that I am a "healer," only to convince people that the sound *they* produce with their own voices can have an effect upon their bodies.

The Tone does not have to be prolonged or noticeable to people around one. One woman told me that she had a heart condition which caused "catches of pain" and she seemed unable to breathe until she could reach her medication, which often was awkward. "By Toning softly I find relief almost at once. Even if I am riding in a car or bus, or in a room where there is a radio or conversation going on, no one else would be aware of it. If they heard they might just think I was *humming* a little."

This type of Toning is more of an audible deep sigh than verbal. It is always done with the exhaling breath-release-release-release. Toning assists *healing from the inside out*.

Most methods of healing begin on the outside and attempt to reach the trouble. Sometimes the surface is healed but the cause is not removed. Toning releases the health which is natural to the body but which is denied expression by obstructions of the natural flow of energy in the body. This does not deny other means of healing. It just assists the healing process because it is cleansing, harmonious and stimulating to healthy cell growth.

The question arises, "Why doesn't Toning stimulate all cell growth, such as cancer cells?"

Referring to Dr. Tiller's statement about the field, Toning stimulates only that which is natural to the body's field-pattern. We may see it in this way: in a neglected or unoccupied house, dirt, rubbish and mold may accumulate, but when the owners clean it they throw out only the foreign materials, not the furniture and things which belong to them. They restore the house to its proper state.

Toning does this for the body. It cleans the body house of its rubbish and puts it back in right order.

It is well known that a cell will continue to reproduce itself almost endlessly, given proper nutrients, if it is separated from its natural environment in the body. Cancer cells are those cells which for some reason have become independent of the field-pattern of the body, we are told. They have "withdrawn and are doing their own thing," with complete disregard for their relationship to the whole organism. When this action is observed anywhere in nature we find destruction—in physics, a body, humankind's disregard for the environment which results in destruction of natural resources; in society, religion or education. It is becoming more and more evident that any form, a body or structured concept, in order to exist in a healthy, useful manner must follow the Logos; the perfect pattern of the whole. This does not mean that there are no new ways to be found which may lead to improvement but they must be *within the Pattern of Creation* which is based on balance and harmony, if they are to last, and be beneficial as intended.

This is the reason the older cultures, whose evidences we see in the remarkable dimensions of the Pyramid of Giza, Stonehenge, and other places, adhered to mathematical and astronomical calculations. Such structures endured because they were built within the pattern of natural laws.

Every word that we speak, or sound that we make, sets in motion either harmony or discord in our lives. Again, that verse which says, "Not that which goeth into the mouth defileth a man; but that which cometh out of the mouth, this defileth a man," can have new meaning. Idle words, sharp sarcastic words, hostile and fearful words leave their mark upon us. That is why we should avail ourselves of a daily Tone bath.

Take a Moment

- It is time for a quick Tone shower.

- Imagine you are under a shower of sound. Let a "hum" or "ah" descend over your head, neck, shoulders, torso and whole body.

- With every inhalation, bring fresh "imaginary" sound to balance and soothe your mind and body.

"You will be a failure, until you impress the subconscious with the conviction you are a success."

— FLORENCE SCOVEL SHINN

CHAPTER 5

The Need for Daily Toning

by Laurel Elizabeth Keyes

THE NEED FOR DAILY TONING may be better understood when we have a clearer picture of how the vibrations of thought, emotions and voice relate to the body and why they have such a strong influence upon us.

As you probably know, we have a colloidal system, along with all the other wonderful mechanisms of our being. The word *colloid* comes from the Greek, meaning *glue*. It constitutes the connecting link between the psychic nature and the physiological organism.

From atom to molecule to colloid, we are dealing with energy vortexes. A small speck seen under a microscope is a thousand times larger than a colloid—which, like the atom, is not a "thing" but a unit of energy. Yet, each of these is a tiny universe with the same functioning as a solar system. (These assertions are made through the ability of science to register the wavelengths and frequencies and measure them mathematically.)

If we take the sphere of a substance, a drop of water for instance, and make two spheres of the substance, the volume of the two will be equal to the one but the surface dimensions of the two smaller spheres will be greater than the surface of the larger one. The smaller the units, the greater becomes the surface area.

The surface of vast numbers of colloids contained in a sphere the size of a #10 buckshot is estimated to equal about one-half acre. Or, to give a picture of this to your subconscious mind to grasp, if you took your fingernails and rolled them into little balls, there would be enough colloidal surface contained in them to spread over a city block.

How many such little balls do you think your body contains? This will give you some idea of the immense area contained within you; probably thousands of acres of quivering, sensitive "glue" which holds you together, but which can be disturbed by the smallest vibration from feeling or sound!

And while colloids are an energy system, when conditions cause them to "condense" they pass into a crystalloid state that becomes form. That is why emotions and sound disturbing the colloidal level eventually manifest in the physical body.

Every thought that you and everyone else thinks has its force in energy. Every feeling that you and others have is thrown into the energy frequencies. We exist in an ocean of positive and negative forces and we could easily drown if it were not for the protection we have in establishing control of our colloidal system through the proper voice tones. These form and concentrate the patterns of our fields. And, if I understand Dr. Tiller's theory correctly, the colloidal energy is the "substance" of the field.

It is evident from this that no one can afford to indulge in emotional storms, anger, fear, self-pity and such negative influences, or identify with or react to them when expressed by others.

"Thought-feeling forces have profound influence in terms of electromagnetic energy upon the surface tensions of the colloids. When one permits inharmonious frequencies to register on the colloidal surface, it goes negative. Other positive forces will register on the negative and will affect the structure of the protoplasmic phase in the configurating process and will ultimately become crystalloid—that is, organic entities which we label tumors, cancer, and other illness. That is the end product of what begins in the colloidal world.

"It is so important that the surface of the colloidal field be positively charged. And it is very simple: maintain enthusiasm. When you pour love and interest into whatever you are doing, you are automatically insulating this field against inharmonious conditions. Internal harmony is an insulator against external inharmony."[7]

Toning, chanting, verbal prayer, all of these direct the voice in calmness and confidence, giving the needed positive charge to the miles of "glue" surface. It impresses ripples of enthusiasm and joy upon the field, in morning Toning, and makes it an invisible armor for your day.

Each day in the cloisters of our individual lives, we can use a breath and sound method to cleanse our bodies and fields. This applies to problems as well as healing.

After the initial morning Toning, sit comfortably with your back straight, head erect. Close your eyes and inwardly watch your breath slow to about four times a minute.

Visualize a pure white light, such as sunlight on snow, pouring in through the top of your head. Feel it go down the spine and out through the nerves to every part of your body. Inhale this light. Think of yourself as attached to "The Father" by this cord of Light. Through its pulsations, as you breathe, you are formed, sustained and give birth to consciousness of your divine nature. Through your mother you were born on the physical level. Through this divine Father you are born on the level of consciousness.

You become aware of your rightful heritage; that you need not be a slave to the circumstances (which you have created through ignorance) but can be a master of the world you create with your ideas, feelings and voice.

With each breath that you inhale feel this light flooding through you from above, down your spine, out through the nerves to every portion of your body. *Feel,* "With every breath I inhale I am renewed and restored in the perfection in which I was created." Feel your body fill with light.

With each breath that you exhale, visualize this changed to a cool, violet cleansing light flowing up through and around you, dissolving all of the shadows and problems in your life. Make a soft humming sound and feel, "With every breath that I exhale, I release all imperfections and the memory of every unpleasant experience, and I am left cleansed, healed and filled with peace."

Practice this for as long as convenient. It should be at least ten minutes.

For the need of the subconscious to see pictures, visualize a cup of black ink in which you let clear water drop a drop at a time. Let it dilute and replace the ink until you eventually have the cup filled with clean water. Each breath can help cleanse your body of impurities. This is not just an idea of the mind. You are *feeling* the breath enter your nostrils and go into your body so the subconscious realizes that *something is happening.* Therefore it may expect a result—change. It has entered into the process and some of its will is being released to your guidance.

Now draw a deep breath, keeping the visualization of the scintillating, healing power of the light going down the spine and out through the nerves, and direct it to any affected or painful area.

Hold your breath there, feeling that you are forcing life to heal there. Feel the throb as you concentrate on that area. Then, exhale suddenly with a groan and feel the breath force out any imperfection from those cells, and that they are freed for their normal expression or healthy growth. Feel the light increase in that place as you visualize the "divine fire" in the nucleus of the cells devour any germ or intruder. (This is called *bonfiring.* The more trash heaped upon a bonfire, the brighter the blaze.)

One of the ways to feel in control of pain, at least to have periods of freedom from it, is to use this breath and sound method. Draw in the breath and force it to the area of pain and feel the breath *push out,* or flush out the pain. It seems to leave as long as the breath is held, and then released in this manner.

With each exhalation, the intensity of the pain appears to diminish, for the subconscious mind has accepted the picture of the diluted ink in the cup and *expects* less pain to remain after each breath is released. It is being washed away.

A person dying with terminal cancer told me that "The greatest pain was the fear that I had no control over it. That nothing more could be done. That the medication would wear out and I would be helpless in the agony of suffering. But, when a friend brought me the Toning book and I began groaning and using the breath to hold out the pain, I gained a wonderful confidence that I could do something to control it. Even if I can hold it out for just a few seconds, it gives me comfort."

The power of the voice, with the mind-feeling-breath, is a vast, almost unexplored realm in our Western culture. The voice is so important because not only does *it set the pattern of our life, it gives us the use of the will to live it.*

In speaking, Toning or chanting, with knowing and conviction, we are able to bring oneness to our divided nature. We are made whole.

This applies to problems as well as the need for healing. When one feels discouraged, inadequate, frustrated, fearful—any negative condition—the transforming change begins the moment one stands up, pulls up the ribcage, breathes deeply and sends the voice out with the authority to correct the condition.

We are the most magnificent creations of which we know. Surely it was intended that we have control over our lives and live in the perfection intended for us; without, of course, causing any harm to another. When one experiences the blessed benefits from Toning, using it in a destructive manner would be unthinkable. Life, which is the moving force of all energy, has a beautiful regulator. It amounts to this: *Whatever is wrongfully used will return to destroy the user.* The voice which embodies feelings of violence, hatred or selfish power will attract those qualities back.

Such a one is setting in motion their own self-destruction.

We cannot change the order of the planets about the sun, nor the affairs of the planet upon which we live, but we can move in harmony with the patterns that regulate that energy, and within our own lives become a sun which governs events and circumstances in our private worlds. We were made to identify with the light rather than fight or surrender to the shadows.

"In the beginning was the Word."

In the end we become the words we speak.

Take a Moment

- Observe your body and mind. Notice if there is any tension or discomfort.

- Begin an "aaah" sound and let the tone release the tension.

- Experiment with your voice as you release energy.

- After five or six tonal exhalations, rest and reflect on harmony.

- Stretch before you begin the next chapter.

"You are today where your thoughts have brought you; you will be tomorrow where your thoughts take you."

— JAMES ALLEN

CHAPTER 6

Results from Toning

by Laurel Elizabeth Keyes

THE PIONEER WORK in Toning has been done by the Fransisters, a group of women with varying backgrounds and lifestyles who have met weekly for a period of years to study and serve.

When I first discovered the benefits of Toning in 1960, our little Fransister group had the aspiration to go out and heal everyone in the world. And the world heard about it and came quickly to be healed.

We received requests, by letter and phone, from people in all parts of the country—and miraculous things happened, not only in healing but in other areas. Jobs were found. New clothes arrived. All manner of situations were changed.

But without *the person's own effort to recognize the cause and remove it,* they became as dependent upon our Toning as upon a drug. This is not healing. It may be helpful and comforting, but is considered temporary, as medicine, surgery or other treatment is unless the cause is corrected.

Usually an illness is the result of breaking some natural law, improper diet, emotional upheavals, nervous or physical exhaustion, tensions, and the like. And while Toning for them could aid, and relieve pain, the real healing should come from within themselves.

We had to let it be known that we would teach people to Tone for themselves but we could no longer run a first-aid station.

However, in our early experiences we had assurance that the forces of visualization, feeling and sound used in Toning could produce remarkable results.

We have been awakened at night to Tone for a stranger a thousand miles away, and relief was reported. We have seen X-rays of the healing of bones (miraculously) when amputation had been considered the only means of saving a life. Certainly the sound does not travel across the miles, or through the earth, yet results are there. We are using some natural force which is not generally recognized yet.

In the beginning, when frowning intellectuals asked me how many control experiments we had done to "prove" this theory, I was happy to reply, "None. We haven't felt the need, nor had the time to waste, to prove something that we find works. We just go ahead and use it."

I do believe that Dr. Tiller has explained how it works in his paper on nodal points extending from a field. "To be in resonance with any one of these points, is to be in resonance with the particular gland of the entity."[8]

One of our first demonstrations was Toning for a young woman who stopped off in Denver, feeling too ill to continue her flight on to New York. She had the flu and a very stiff neck, she was exceedingly weak since she had not been able to eat for several days, and she had a violent headache. As she slumped in a chair before us, she appeared to be a most miserable and helpless person.

Two of us Toned for her for about fifteen minutes. I had been standing with my hands, palms together (as in a prayer position) just under my chin. I felt a power build up in my hands as I Toned and I said to the woman as I walked over and stood in front of her, "Ask what you want but be sure you want it. I feel it will be released to you." (I had never done that before and I was acting entirely on intuition.)

She didn't open her eyes. She mumbled, "I want to be free of this pain and sickness, and whatever caused it."

I opened my hands and held them, palms out, toward her.

She convulsed in the chair as though she had received an electrical shock.

She sat up and asked, "What happened?"

We could not answer. We stood with our mouths open, too surprised to speak. One thing that I had been taught was "Never let fear in, no matter what you are doing." If we could have, we would have been frightened, but we just stood watching.

The woman sat up straight, twisted her head from side to side freely, amazed.

"It's free. No pain. What has happened? I feel wonderful."

Then she stood up, walked about the room and kept saying, "I feel so wonderful. I can't believe it. I don't believe in miracles. This can't have happened, but I feel *wonderful*. There isn't a pain or ache anywhere. I never felt better. And, I'm hungry."

She said she felt as though she were walking on air. We drove her to the airport and while we waited for her plane she ordered a large lunch and ate it all with relish. She kept asking, "What happened?"

We, being new in working with Tone, could only say, "We'll try to find out. We are as astonished as you are." She told us later that she retained that exalted feeling the rest of that day and night and into the next day, when after working at her office she felt "normal" again. All symptoms of the illness were gone.

What had happened? At that time we guessed that in Toning we had helped her body release the tensions, and it slipped back and rested in its natural pattern. When I opened my hands, whatever power had been built up there, directed to her, caused her consciousness to be instantly aware of her union with her inner perfection. The results were unexpected, and we were convinced that in Tone there was more power than we had dreamed. It was ours to use; to direct it was within each person's power to use for him or herself as well as for others.

A dentist had a biopsy of an unhealed condition in his lip and found it positive. He made arrangements to have radiation treatment and plastic surgery. But, because the holidays came up and he was very busy, he postponed the treatment for six weeks. In the meantime his wife Toned for his condition and he Toned with her, to humor her, because he was quite sure it could do no good.

Within ten days a scab fell off with tiny hair roots, shriveled, still attached to it. It was as though it had been dried up from the tips of the roots, outward, and "died" from the vibration of the Toning. No treatment was necessary. No scar was left. No recurrence of it after six years.

Another case of skin cancer was that of a woman who had received radiation treatment for it. When it recurred in the same area less than two years later, she Toned. She said that she Toned "violently," causing a resonance to be set up in the area, and continued doing it for thirty minutes at a time for several days. After the first day she said the flesh became swollen and red and had every appearance of having had radiation. "It looked just as it had when I had X-ray treatments." Within a week it was normal again. No recurrence. No other treatment was needed.

A remarkable case was that of a nurse who came to visit her sister. She had lost much of her sight and could no longer read or drive her car. She had been a diabetic for years but because of uremic poisoning could no longer take medication for it. Multiple sclerosis was becoming apparent. She had come to Denver to say goodbye to her family because her doctors could give her no hope for living beyond a few months, and being a nurse she realized the gravity of her condition.

Her sister brought her to see me. She came up the steps, weakly halting at each one, as though she should have been carried in on a stretcher instead of having only the support of her sister's arm.

She fell into a large chair and seemed to melt into it with her pain and hopelessness.

I talked with her for about a half hour, trying to explain Toning, which wasn't easy. Her mind had long been schooled to strict scientific terms. It would be expecting too much to think that I could convince her that anything we could do in a few minutes with our voices could be stronger or more effective than all the known scientific helps, which now had failed. She listened, politely, or perhaps out of exhaustion, and did not protest.

Then her sister and I Toned for her. We Toned for about twenty minutes. We watched her body react as it might have to very mild electrical stimulation. She sat up straighter—a glow began to come to her white cheeks. Then she began to cry.

She cried, great heartbreaking, shaking sobs which were a kind of groaning, really. We encouraged her to cry and we went on Toning.

She said, between the sobbing, "Oh, how I have mistreated my body! I never thought about it except why wouldn't it do more, overworking it, hating it when it wouldn't go on serving me. Forgive me, God—forgive me!"

This was a surprising outburst because she was not a religious person and would not ordinarily have spoken in such a manner. But in the cleansing of the sound, something was released and the healing could begin. Through the crying and in the realization of how she had mistreated her body, and in asking for some power greater than her own to "forgive," she had loosed something held by her subconscious mind.

I took her hands and drew her to her feet, telling her to rise and stand in the new life that had been produced in her.

She did, and she walked around the room with me, briskly, still crying, and then laughing and proclaiming that she felt so much stronger. She walked down the steps unassisted and got into her sister's car without help. I watched, wondering if this would last, or if she would lose it.

Her sister, with whom she was staying, taught her to Tone and for the few days of her remaining visit, they did a good deal of it together.

The woman did not lose her "healing." She continued to Tone when she returned to California. First, the uremic condition cleared up. Her vision improved. She could drive her car again, and read. The multiple sclerosis not only was halted but diminished over the months.

She went to her hospital for tests to be sure that this healing was fact and not a temporary thing. The doctors could not believe it. They had no explanation for it. The facts were that she was free of certain of her ailments and improved in other areas.

Four years later only the diabetic condition remained and that was controlled by medication. She found new enthusiasm in helping build and furnish a mountain cabin. Beyond the physical helps, she had found a new appreciation for her body, and her mental attitude was changed so that she became a much happier person.

Toning is not "faith healing." People who do not believe in it, or do not know that it is being done for them, respond. Plants and animals respond to it. Certainly, they are not using faith. Toning is the right use of natural laws, as in electricity and nuclear power.

A teacher we knew had suffered a pain in his right arm and shoulder for weeks. In spite of medication it continued to grow worse. (His physician had not been able to diagnose the condition and more tests were to be taken.) It had made it impossible for him to write on the blackboard or raise his arm above his head.

We Toned for him, without his knowledge. That evening he was called and asked how he felt.

"The oddest thing happened today," he replied. "For no reason that I know of my arm felt better. I could write on the board, something I've not been able to do for a long time. I can't understand it. The pain is just gone. It's just a little sore but not stiff."

The soreness disappeared within a week and there was no more trouble with the arm. This young man was a very intellectual person and if he had known that we were trying to "heal" him, we were sure that his mind would have rejected it. Since he did not know, he was helped. That is "anti-faith" healing, perhaps?

Then there is the case of the rancher who had "tried everything" and phoned in desperation from Lancaster, California. He had a history of migraine headaches once or twice a week but this one had lasted five days and he was exhausted from the pain. Someone had told him about Toning and he said he was ready to try anything.

"Do you mind the long distance phone bill?" I asked.

"Take as long as you like—just let me get some relief," he answered.

Headaches are difficult to treat because the sound must be soothing or it can accentuate the problem. Since I did not know this man and had never heard from him before, I had to proceed with all of the sensitivity and alertness possible.

Visualization is half of the Toning process. One must reach the subconscious mind with an acceptable impression.

I told the man, "There is an old, inherited body memory of helplessness when blood drains away from it. Use this imagery now. Imagine that you are a bottle, turned upside down, the cork at your feet. Reach down and imagine that you remove the cork and the blood begins to drain out through the bottom of your feet and *feel it*. Feel that you are helpless to stop it. Feel the pain drain away with it—it is slowly draining down from your head, out through your feet—feel it, feel it." (One of the benefits of this is that the attention is put at the other end of the body!)

"Let your breathing slow down—sigh with each breath —let the tensions drain away through your feet—relax, sigh—let go— sigh. Now, groan."

I listened to him, encouraging him to groan more deeply. I groaned with him. "Deeper—louder—sigh," I urged him. And while he listened to the Tone, my voice gently "massaged" his field. I gave an example of letting the voice rise up after feeling the satisfaction of groaning, and soaring free *above* the pain.

When I felt that he had comprehended the process and was able to do it, I told him I would go on Toning for him, while he did it for himself, and we would anticipate complete freedom from the old pain pattern. By this time he felt his headache beginning to subside a little.

"Don't be afraid if you feel a headache coming," I warned him. "Just start groaning. Pull the cork from the bottle and know it will drain away before it can establish itself." (Fear of an approaching migraine causes more tension and hastens the process.)

Two weeks later he wrote a letter.

Everyone at our house is Toning. Even the coyotes who visit our pastures before sunrise in their quest for unwary and foolish ground squirrels. Yes, they tone, and beautifully.

Last Wednesday your tape arrived with the Toning example. It was so calming to listen to. I can't recall when we were so relaxed. Our tensions quickly melted away. Now that we've learned the correct way to groan and to Tone we are feeling better each day. For two weeks my usual migraine has deserted me. And I feel it is going to be a permanent divorce.

I passed the information on to Bill, who works for us. He complained of having painfully clogged sinus cavities. His ear ached and his throat hurt so much that he could hardly swallow, plus his glands down one side of his neck were swollen and so painful he couldn't touch that side of his face.

He had serious doubts that my advice about groaning would help his trouble. In fact, he said his doctor had told him to "hum" to open up his sinuses but instead of clearing them, it had plugged them up! I insisted he give it a try. He said he would and went off to attend to his work.

At lunch he joined us and gleefully reported that he had been Toning while on the tractor and his nose started draining and his sinus cavities no longer pained. He had no earache and his throat and neck had stopped hurting and he was delighted. So were we.

My wife joins me in sending you thoughts of gratitude.

Six months later he felt very confident of his freedom from migraines. He phoned me not long ago to say that during a tension-filled episode in business he felt the old migraine habit starting up but he conquered it quickly, and there has been no recurrence.

An electrical engineer working on outer space projects, one who is in the most modem and foremost fields of scientific exploration, is an ardent Toner. He gives this explanation: "Every morning, and I mean every morning, as I drive to work, I Tone. One benefit is the fantastic workout the lungs receive. Toning actually pushes stale air from the lungs. You get rid of this waste from the lungs without becoming exhausted. Ordinarily to try to exhale and empty the lungs is physically exerting. But, when I Tone it is a slow, steady flow of air, caused by the diaphragm pressure instead of my trying to squeeze it out from outside force. Then the inflow of air rushes in after I exhale. I try to make the feedback loop of breath and Tone so that my body is completely relaxed and I feel that it settles into the Tone. Then I let it ride. Maybe this just lasts for five seconds or so but if I can get into that point where I ride on the Tone and it is a steady Tone, it seems that everything in my body and mind is stilled in perfect union and it gives me a sense of great concentration and power.

"I am not aware of exhaling, or doing anything. My body and my mind and the sound are all one and I have the feeling that I am being carried by this tremendous Power.

"Then I run out of air and take another deep breath, but it

amazes me how long I can 'ride' on this Tone, quite a long time without any effort at all. If I *tried* to take a deep breath and forced it out I couldn't do it nearly as long and I wouldn't feel the benefit I do from Toning.

"It's like driving a car—you start it, put it into neutral and coast. You coast on the sound and you can go a long way on it. That Toning is the most important thing that I do in the morning. I wouldn't go without it. It seems to build a shield around me and anything negative just bounces off before it gets in to me.

"Even if I feel a little tired, or I'm facing a discouraging problem at work, as soon as I Tone everything picks up. It is a mechanical thing. You can't possibly stay 'down' when you Tone, any more than you can stay on the ground floor if you step into an elevator that goes to a top floor."

Now that biofeedback has become well known, and the terms associated with it have become popular in our daily vocabulary, it is helpful to be able to say, "Go into Alpha when you start to Tone." (*Alpha* is the designation given the brainwaves which register on the electroencephalograph machine as approximately 7 to 13 cycles per second. It is below the usual waking, thinking state of *Beta* which ranges from 13 to 28, or more. Below *Alpha* is *Theta*, from about 4 to 7 cycles per second, and that is the area that is exciting exploration now since it appears to be the area where deep intuition functions, miraculous healings, etc. *Delta* is approximately 0 to 4 cycles and is deep sleep or unconsciousness.)

I have had the privilege of being tested by Dr. Elmer and Alyce Green at Menninger's and found that Toning produced Alpha waves almost at once. Theta could be reached by deep quietness but I found it extremely interesting that I could also register Theta when I kept my mind "still" but felt an inner enthusiasm; what I termed "contained anticipation." This may have been touching one of the deeper states of meditation which the Indian yogis experience. It is a deep inner awareness that is greatly sharpened, not by "thinking" but by "being." And, I have noticed at times when Toning for others that this Theta does happen. There is so much yet to be explored and found in these areas of functioning. Nothing we can find in outer space can ever equal the wonders that we may discover in our inner space.

Toning helps us to feel our inner peace through release. We release health from within as a flower is released from the pattern in the seed. We release willpower as we release the positive feelings of our highest and best intentions. And, we release hope, confidence, love and joyousness—all of these qualities native to the soul, as we let our voice express its freedom.

Take a Moment

- Think of Toning as release.

- First, release all tension, pressure and blockage (through groaning) which prevents the natural, healthy expression of life forces.

- Second, release the vital force contained in one's field, according to its pattern of perfection.

"There came a time when the risk to remain tight in the bud was more painful than the risk it took to blossom."

— ANAIS NIN

CHAPTER 7

Toning for Others

by Laurel Elizabeth Keyes

WHEN WE TONE for others we begin by doing the daily Toning ritual until we feel in perfect balance. We close our eyes for better concentration and Tone the name of the person. It has been determined that the natural tone range of the human voice is from A below middle C to A above. We hold the idea of the quality of each note as we progress upward.

A *The Absolute,* Creative Force undifferentiated— the One.

B *Descension* into dense form; the animal and plant level of manifestation.

C *Purification* of that form—the turning point, out of the animal level toward the divine.

D *Vitality.* Here the human begins to form and vitality is given to it. (Interesting to note that our vitamin D gives vitality, C, an infection fighter, etc., yet these qualities to sound were given thousands of years before we named vitamins.)

E *Harmony,* a bringing together of the lower and higher natures in peace. It is as "salve to the wounds." Healing.

F *Formation.* F is said to be the great Tone of Nature. Visualize the perfect form to be manifested. We are reminded that what is visualized while F is being sounded must be perfection. Do not see a person in bed with an illness while Toning in F—you will only add power to the illness. See the person well, going about daily life, free of limitation.

G *Gratitude.* Now that the "new" form has been made, rejoice. Let it live through gratitude. "Gratitude is the highest form of prayer" because it is a release, an out-rushing of positive force, lifting one as it goes.

A *Completion* (above middle C) The cycle is now completed from the unconscious Life force to conscious union with the inner Potential. It is "one with the Father," in Christian terms. One is consciously raising one's "self" from the imprisonment in animal instincts, habits, fears, and so on, to a masterful and happy direction of life.

This cycle of Toning, followed with the visualization as given, is a daily lifting and conquering. It is re-living the traditional story of consciousness "falling" into lower state functioning, then the purification and return to full potential of human achievement, and joy.

As sleep is said to be the "little daily death," so does Toning in this manner give a pattern of the "little daily resurrection"; a taste of immortality.

A psychiatrist told me, "The basic urge in the human is to worship. This urge is deeper than the sex urge, it is experienced from the infant stage to the very aged. The human must look to something greater than he is, something in which he can feel secure because he believes it to be right, changeless, wise, powerful and eternal. He must have such a Power to trust or he does not have an urge to progress. To cut off this need to worship is like cutting the main root of a tree. It then becomes top-heavy and falls. So will mankind become over-mentalized and fall if he does not sustain himself with the nourishment of worship." But worship in its complete sense is to have union with that which is worshiped. For full satisfaction we must DO something to become worthy of, to be similar, to be "one with" the worshiped.

By Toning this cycle daily one assures the subconscious mind that one has control of one's life and *can* change imperfections. One can lift oneself to better living—*he is doing it* by lifting his voice from A to A. It is a symbol *experienced*. It is a conviction to the subconscious mind because it can be *felt*.

To be sure we are hitting the note accurately, we use a small chromatic pitch instrument. (It is about the size of a thin yo-yo and we carry it in our pockets and use it frequently during the day.)

Toning the name of the person is first, purification, then healing, then gratitude (acceptance) that the healing is already at work. We seldom Tone for a person more than once. If it is done properly, once should be enough. We who are sensitive seem to have a type of sonar which causes us to "know" when the person has been reached and is healed. Time after time in our little group, we will Tone for some person and then we will ask what each one felt about the person. The majority receive the same impression. I have been asked to Tone for people about whom I knew nothing, not even the nature of the illness. In Toning this sonar system has been verified in enough instances to make me believe it could not possibly be coincidence.

We are not doing a miraculous thing in Toning. We are simply relaxing the person into their natural state of health. Toning may only be the removal of whatever obstruction has crept into the person's "field."

It must be recognized that illness is the result of some discord in the field, and we should look for the cause. "When an illness comes we know that it is a time when the Father tenderly gathers us closer to Him to tell us something we have been doing wrong, or need to correct, or learn. Sometimes we grow so busy (we think) that we forget how much we need the Grace of union with our divine nature.

"Someone calls and we rush to answer, and another and another, and without realizing it we find that God has been calling and we did not hear Him in the multitude of sounds.

"Then He draws us close, through what we call a problem or illness. And, we listen. In illness, we are forced to listen; to take time to re-evaluate our lives and to sort out the important from the superfluous. Were it not for these periods we might not begin to unfurl the tight little leaves of our spiritual potentialities," so wrote the Founder of the Fransisters.

Each of us can feel secure only when we know that we need not rely upon any outside agent; by releasing the Life within us, we are healed. That is why we encourage the practice of daily Toning.

An amusing example of the old saying, "God will help you out of a difficulty once, but if you repeat the mistake, you'll have to get out by yourself," occurred in our group.

One of our Fransisters knew how to Tone and had healed many minor ailments but she did not pay attention to warning signals of overwork and she contracted pneumonia. Strong medication was administered, and with Toning, she recovered quickly.

The next year, after a similar period of overwork, there were signs of pneumonia recurring. The same medication was ineffective. She was forced to rely upon Toning.

She managed to get out of bed, and as she stood gasping, she began to Tone. She said it was like "pulling her will up by its bootstraps," but up it came. Two hours later she was able to drive out into a snow storm to keep an appointment; and that was the end of the illness.

We do not suggest such drastic self-treatment for beginners. *Do not depend upon what you have not proved.* This is mentioned only as an example of how we may grow careless and repeat mistakes, and are jerked back to proper functioning.

In other ways than illness, Toning is very effective.

A landlord rented a house to some people who falsely represented themselves and when they were given notice to move, they caused a great deal of trouble and threatened a lawsuit. He did not argue with them. He went home and Toned. He saw them out of his house and going to a place better suited for them. "What is good for one is good for all concerned," is the proper attitude for Toning in such situations.

When he went back to the house three days later he found that they had moved. Nothing more had been said to them. Perhaps Toning "gave them an idea" that they did not want to stay and go through the unpleasantness of legal action.

Another case was that of a teacher whose behavior had been considered detrimental to students. For four years parents had signed petitions and tried to have the teacher removed. He had tenure. He would sue the school board, he said, for prejudice and other false claims.

A mother, moving into that community and feeling that her children were going to be deprived of their proper education, began Toning.

She Toned, seeing the teacher's chair empty. That was all—no resentment, no anger—just that his chair was empty and that he was drawn to a place where he would be happier, for surely no one could be happy where he knew he was not wanted.

In the middle of the school year, about a month later, the teacher suddenly announced that he was "fed up with the West" and he was going back to civilization in the East. And, he left.

Toning does work. It is not manipulating people, or exerting power over people—the idea is simply to restore people to their harmonic patterns.

Frequently I am the most surprised at the results from Toning. I expect miracles, but what form they will take I do not guess.

I was invited to speak to a group of patients at a mental hospital near Denver.

"Do not be dismayed if there is no response," I was told. "This is a group of chronic cases which have been under treatment for from three to five years. We try to get them to relate to outside interests, but so far they have not responded to group therapy or any of our standard methods."

To get some idea of other subjects they had had I inquired what their last guest had used as a topic.

"We had an official of the telephone company explain dialing and how messages are relayed." (What that had to do with mental health I couldn't imagine, but I did not think it was an act that would be hard to follow.)

I had spoken to inmates at the State Prison, and heard the gates clank behind me in the psychiatric ward at Colorado General Hospital when I went there to speak, and remembered one of the patients saying as I left, "Can't we have her again? I could understand *her.*" Whether that was complimentary or not it gave me confidence for this encounter.

I passed patients sitting in the parlors and in the halls, slouched over, cigarettes or coke bottles in their hands, eyes on the floor—waiting. Waiting for something to happen to make life worth living again.

About twenty-five men and women were seated in a circle in a large room. That was my audience. Two white uniformed attendants were in the back of the room. I was introduced. No one cared who I was or why I was there. They sat, shoulders bent, eyes staring at the floor.

To get past their mental shells I knew that I must reach the subconscious mind—touch some remembered experience with absurd picturization. I began telling very corny jokes about myself. A head or two came up and eyes looked at me. I seemed to be having such fun that they smiled back at me. Soon there were more heads raised and more smiles. There was interest. It had taken a full twenty minutes out of my allotted hour and a half but it was encouraging. I was using my voice as a lever to pry them up!

I introduced them to groaning. They liked it and a great jumble of sounds began to come out. An attendant disappeared and returned with two more personnel. By then I had the patients on their feet and we began Toning. They were responding! All except one woman who grabbed her coke bottle and walked out defensively.

While they sat down to rest after our vigorous Toning I explained to them, "We make the mistake of identifying with our thoughts. We think our thoughts are reality. They are made of dream stuff. You can't be satisfied by *remembering* eating last Thanksgiving's turkey if you're hungry. It's not real. Memories aren't real, we just think they are. We forget that WE ARE THE THINKER AND WE CAN CHANGE OUR THOUGHTS. And, if we can change our thoughts, and feelings, we can change our world because we make our own world out of memories and opinions and thought-stuff."

A doctor interrupted. "Isn't that being unrealistic? Isn't that rather a Pollyanna approach?"

"What was wrong with Pollyanna? She was happy, wasn't she?" I countered. "Of course we fool ourselves in almost all sense-perceptions. We see the sun rise at a certain time and it hasn't 'risen' at all. We have turned towards it. We hear the sound of a plane in one place in the sky and see the plane somewhere else, where it has traveled before the sound reached our ears. But, let's have sense enough to fool ourselves happy instead of sad. It's our life. Let's make it fun." I spoke in such simple terms for the patients' benefit.

I asked the patients to close their eyes and feel the chairs upon which they were seated, so they could describe them to me if I asked. When they opened their eyes again I told them, "You thought that the chair was smooth, and cool, because that is how you thought it felt. But you didn't feel the chair. *You felt the feeling* in your hand; that sensation triggered a memory in your brain and you *thought* the chair was smooth or cool. The smooth-cool was in your brain, wasn't it?"

Obviously, some of them could not grasp it but I kept trying. "Now, compared to very fine silk that chair would seem rough, wouldn't it? Compared to dry ice, that chair would feel warm, wouldn't it? You see, things are not fixed—not just one way; they are only what you think they are. You are the THINKER, not the thought, and you can change your thoughts about anything. You are the boss of your mind. Make it serve you and do what you want it to do. Now, let's think we're going to have fun."

I got them on their feet again and we did a dance, stomping and shouting a lot of "Hi-ya, hi-ya-hi-ya, HI," sounds. We were behaving like children, and having a good time.

I looked at the several doctors and attendants in the back of the room. I couldn't resist inviting them to join us—and they didn't dare refuse! It was so comical to see them, too, marching along like Indians, yelling and stomping. We did it until we were breathless and most of the patients were laughing with me.

Many of the patients crowded around me, asking me when I could come back again. "Tomorrow?" they suggested. They liked it.

One man, probably in his late thirties, took my hand and looked me squarely in the eyes and said, "You have changed my life today. I've made institutions a way of life because I thought the outside world was just too tough for me. Today, when you made me see that I am the 'thinker and not the thought' I got the feeling that I can't waste any more time. Maybe life is a game that I'd enjoy playing. Thank you, and God bless you."

"Good," I told him. "Get in there and play to win."

Six months later I was invited back. This time there wasn't a doctor in sight. (They must have heard that I was coming?)

I asked the attendant who was directing me to the right room, "Is this the same group to whom I spoke last time?"

"No," she said brightly, "they have gone into cottages now. This is another group."

They had "graduated" into cottage living after one Toning session? However, there was more to it than that. When I had been there before I had asked how much physical exercise they were given each day, and had been told, "Once a week we have a twenty-minute exercise period."

I must have shown my astonishment clearly. "But they need healthy bodies for restored minds."

I had suggested at least that much exercise every day, with additional singing, folk dancing, interpretative dancing—anything that would combine movement and voice and move them out of those dull ruts of just sitting and talking or thinking about their problems. Such a program had been instituted and undoubtedly it had contributed to the patients' improvement.

"Do you remember the man who talked to you the last time you were here?" the nurse asked.

"Yes. Will I see him today?"

"No, he has left us. That is the message he wanted me to give to you. He has a position now. He is a physicist, you know. He wanted me to tell you how much you had helped him, and that he is 'winning.'"

If only one mind had found its freedom from its self-imposed imprisonment, it had been more than worth the effort I had put forth that day. It was another miracle from Toning.

When we become aware of our voice and its influence on other people, we realize that the person who speaks in harsh, bellicose tones causes hostility to flare in return. One who speaks from weakness invites imposition and endless problems. A person who speaks with consideration and kindness finds a similar response from others. Most of all, *as we speak we influence ourselves.*

Take a Moment

• Reflect on sending mental tones to a friend or a family member. Notice your breath and enjoy the release of energy being given to them with each exhalation.

• Experiment with the Toning Cycle described early in the chapter.

"Kindness in words creates confidence.
Kindness in thinking creates profound-
ness. Kindness in giving creates love."

— LAO TZU

CHAPTER 8

Miraculous Healing

by Laurel Elizabeth Keyes

EVERY LIVING THING has its pattern of perfection upon which it was formed. The grass seed, the fruit, the flower, the pattern of the bird in its egg, and humans—all have their patterns.

It is natural, therefore, to be healthy and happy. If there are malformations or disease it is an indication that something has disturbed the pattern. Healing is a matter of removing the debris, or coating, which hinders the natural flow of light expanding outward from the nucleus. Today scientists are studying the DNA factor, the inherited pattern within the cells of the body. Their studies have led them into experimentation with sound vibrations and cellular reactions.

Dr. William Tiller defines one aspect of healing which explains to me how sound vibrations, such as Toning, "loaded with an image," can be effective.

A basic idea in radionics is that each individual, organism or material radiates and absorbs energy via a unique wave field which exhibits certain geometrical frequency and radiation-type characteristics. This is an extended force field that exists around all forms of matter whether animate or inanimate. A useful analogy here is the physical atom that is continually radiating electromagnetic energy in the form of waves because of its oscillating electric dipole moment and its thermal vibrations... Regions of space associated with a given phase angle of the wave constitute a three dimensional network of points in resonance with the particular gland of the entity. The capability of scanning the waveform of the gland exists for the detection of any abnormalities. Likewise, if *energy* having the normal or healthy waveform of the gland is pumped into any of these specific network points, *the gland will be driven in the normal or healthy mode.* This produces a tendency for its structure to reorganize itself in closer alignment with the normal structure; healing of the gland occurs. Cells born in the presence of this polarizing field tend to grow in a healthier configuration which weakens the original field of the abnormal or diseased structure and strengthens the field of the normal or healthy structure.[9] [italics added]

It was believed in the ancient Mystery Teachings that the nucleus of every human cell was formed around the seed atom which was Spirit and in that nucleus was contained the pattern of its perfection.

Healing meant the release of that perfection so that it was evident in the body.

There was another factor which was associated with that fire of the Spirit. That was Will. Will was divine. It was life. It was God. In Western religious writings we are reminded often of the "Will of God," and "the Father's Will," and the free will which apparently causes all of our problems.

Will was the spirit of God which moved life into manifestation. It was the activator in creation. If it operated unhampered, all was as it should be and peace resulted.

But back there somewhere when the divine consciousness (image-making ability) came into the animal form, the sensations of the animal nature began to steal the imagination process and use this power of the will separate from the instinctive governing factors of the animal nature.

The subconscious mind gained control of the will and held it jealously, for through it, it had greater power. Referring to the soul-mind-body relationship, the body now controlled the mind with the willpower it had usurped from the soul, and separated the body's functioning from the soul's direction. Authority had shifted and chaos resulted.

We see the picture of the animal nature which has stolen the power without having the ability to use it wisely, and so would misuse it and destroy itself. (Our discovery of atomic energy is a comparable analogy. New and enormous power came into our use but we have lacked the wisdom to use it properly and we live in danger of annihilation.)

To objectify it we may visualize a chimpanzee which stole the keys to the car of its keeper. By imitating things it had seen the keeper do, it started the car and drove it at full speed until it crashed. Then, sitting bewildered and possibly hurt, it looked back and sought the help of its keeper.

To live in health and peace we must convince the subconscious mind to let the Keeper operate our vehicle. We must loosen its hold on willpower.

Since it has control of our willpower it follows that the "stolen will" must be relinquished back to the Perfect Will for healing to manifest.

This requires the feeling of surrender. But it must be understood that the surrender is to the Perfection and *not to the illness*.

So often people who are ill and hope for spiritual healing will say, "I have surrendered to God's Will." God's Will could never be anything but perfection. They surrender—but to the disease or problem instead, becoming resigned and negative about it.

A beautiful example of proper surrender is that of a young woman who was told that she had cancer and without surgery could live only a very few months. She had a small baby and two other youngsters— and a religious conviction that God would heal. She resisted the pleas of her husband, family and friends, even her minister, to have surgery. "I stood naked in my faith and utterly alone but I was convinced that God would heal me and if He wouldn't I didn't want to live. I never *felt* doubt."

Her surrender was not to the illness but to the perfection of His Will. Even when she was so ill that she could spend only short periods out of bed she felt that the healing was happening underneath the pain.

All during the summer she kept that lonely vigil of faith and on Thanksgiving Day a violent physical reaction occurred. "There was an emptying, a cleansing of my body from the bowels and mouth," she wrote, "which seemed to leave me absolutely hollow and filled with light. It was the most vile, awful stuff that came out, but as soon as it stopped I began to feel stronger and well."

I have her letter written just before Christmas of that year, containing a copy of her doctor's report. "After extensive laboratory tests, we find no cancer cells present." That, she wrote, was the Father's Christmas present to her.

That was four years ago and a recent letter stated that she is enjoying excellent health.

Her surrender was total but it was to the image of health in which she had been created. She identified with that image. Each day she thanked God for healing. A common misunderstanding of prayer is that when we pray *for* something to come to us, or to happen to us, we are causing the subconscious mind to *acknowledge separation from it.* And that which we seek is held out and away from us. That is why reference is made in the Bible to "pray with thanksgiving." Pray as though what is sought is *already here.* This programs the subconscious mind to accept that image instead of the picture of the lack.

I do not encourage anyone who has any fear or doubt to follow this young woman's example but I do want to relate the case because it can happen, it does happen when the conscious mind completely convinces the subconscious that its true nature is perfect.

Not all people who claim to have faith are healed and this is the source of so much anguish. Why doesn't it work for everyone who tries it?

I have attended gatherings of thousands where the people came in wheelchairs, on crutches, in desperation, believing, trusting and having faith. Out of five thousand people perhaps eighty or one hundred were healed. That is a very small percentage, it seems, for an all-loving and powerful heavenly Father to heal. Surely, more than that number believed that they had faith. A human parent does not say to a child, "You will be healed, but you I will not heal; you must continue to suffer," when the child cries out for help.

This cannot be explained away as divine whim or as a divine mystery that "we are not supposed to understand." I believe that we can understand it. At least we must make the effort to find answers.

Even more puzzling to the faithful is the fact that many unbelievers are healed at such meetings. A typical example is one which I witnessed where two women whom I knew attended. One had a slight diabetic condition, the other had a severe arthritic condition in her knee. The diabetic went out of curiosity. It didn't occur to her to ask for healing because she hadn't thought about it happening to her. She was occupied with thinking of a relative whom she should have brought because that person might have been healed. She was completely unconscious of herself. Suddenly "something like a mild shock" went through her and the Evangelist on the platform looked down her way and said, "Three women have been healed of diabetes. Go to your doctors tomorrow and have tests. You have been healed." Later she did go and there was no trace of diabetes.

The girl with the faith, an ardent believer who had dedicated her life to spiritual service, had prayed fervently. Nothing happened. She still has her stiffened leg.

Miraculous healings are not outside of natural law, only outside of humanity's limited understanding. They are evidence, rather, of the powers available to us which most people do not know how to accept.

While I have been writing this manuscript a woman phoned to tell me of the "miracle" in her life. She had come to see me a couple of months before. She was in her middle thirties and much too young for the arthritis which was afflicting her arms and hands. Her story suggested why it might have appeared. She had been a professional pianist but her husband (a second marriage which she felt must not fail) objected to her playing. He had a violent temper, she said, and criticized her about everything she did, including keeping house and caring for the children. She became depressed, ill, had terrible headaches and spent much of her time in bed.

We had a Toning session and I explained to her how to vitalize her field with hope and enthusiasm, and to use her voice in a positive manner instead of the negative tone. I had heard nothing from her until this phone call. "I can't believe the change in our lives. I never said a word to my husband but I began practicing what you told me. I felt better. My headaches stopped. I began to play again and enjoy my housework and last night my husband came in and said, 'I don't know what has changed you but you are certainly a different person. It's a joy to think of coming home to you at the end of the day. You're so bright and cheerful and you're baking again and making a real home for the kids and me.'"

She finished by saying, "I've been a Christian all of my life and prayed, but until you explained things to me I never knew *how* to let the Father's Will work in my life."

Why does a miracle touch some lives, and not others?

It appears that whether the healings result from Christian beliefs, Indian sand paintings, Shaman's rituals, in Hindu temples or Sufi, for the most part they have two things evidenced. Sound (music, singing, chanting or vocal prayers) and body movement (clapping, dancing, stomping, kneeling, etc.). A powerful field of psychic or kinetic energy is built up by the audience or person. Static electricity can be built up in fabric during a wind storm; touching a doorknob after walking across a rug can give an electric shock. *The field is there. Contact with it releases the power.*

When this happens in the body we call it a miraculous healing.

Some may be skeptical and declare such healings are mass hypnotism or hysteria. It is much more than that. In the sense that all healings, as all beauty, harmony and love, are of divine origin, it is creative force in form.

This energy lies latent in all people in the patterns of our cells. Seldom is it given opportunity to be expressed because the conscious mind blocks it with doubt or denial and the subconscious, through its blind urges, fear or old traumatic experiences, bars the door to its release.

Many of the people who attend healing meetings go as a last

resort. They have tried many other types of treatment and experienced repeated disappointments. The subconscious holds those memories. It does not want to be fooled again with vain hopes. It will not be convinced. It will not surrender its will to some uncertain authority again. It reacts from memory. It knows what *has* happened. It cannot imagine what has *not* happened. So, the trusting person with faith, perhaps faith beyond a mental conviction, can't unlock the hold that the subconscious mind retains.

In the case of the two women: The one who was healed was not doubting, she was only curious. Curiosity opens wide the door of the mind. Feeling-wise she was not involved so she was not rejecting it. Her subconscious had nothing to fear. She was wishing her relative were there. In that charged atmosphere where loud singing had gone on for two hours and the frequency had been raised with anticipation, excitement and enthusiasm, her conscious mind was totally removed from herself (she was thinking of someone else) and her subconscious mind was overpowered by the energy field. It relaxed—and the Pattern of Perfection was released in a healing.

This is one of the reasons that praying for another often permits our own prayer to be answered. We catch our subconscious off guard and the Divine Will takes control.

Another instance of this is that of a young woman in her mid-thirties with an arthritic spine that promised no future but a wheelchair. Pat had a baby and two other small children, but even with her affliction she could not resist helping others who had "greater afflictions" of having no faith or spiritual awareness. She took a girl into her home to help. The girl had an unbelievable background, beginning in the slums where she had to fight to live—for bread and for her body. Pat was the first person she had found who loved her and asked nothing in return. Just loved her. She was nursed back to health and self-respect and a bright future was ahead.

When the time came for the girl to leave, with her new husband, she came to Pat to thank her and say goodbye.

Pat wrote, "I had found that Toning could help me live with pain. While I was Toning, and for a short time thereafter, I would have a 'breathing spell.' Jean had come in while I was kneeling, Toning. We had Toned for ourselves and others. We had now entered our quiet time of meditation when we sought guidance, grace, courage, peace, whatever was needed to fill the perfection of our souls.

"Suddenly, I began to experience a strange sensation. I felt as though I was in a vortex of violent whirling. It seemed that every atom of my body had joined with the other atoms and that they all were whirling at a terrific speed in something of a spiral going around and up. I cannot say how long this lasted. I was not dizzy, yet I could not have moved. I knew that whatever was taking place within or upon my body was good. But, I could not comprehend what was happening.

"Then I knew! As the whirling sensation was going up and up, each joint was giving its pain into the whirl of light. What was left was the feeling that each joint was now resting upon a cushion of air rather than grinding bone against bone. An unbounded joy began to fill me.

"The whirl was still going. I tried my voice, not sure that it would work. It did. I didn't attempt to open my eyes or even to move. 'Jean' I said, 'the most extraordinary thing is happening to me.'

"'What?' came her tense reply.

"As best I could I tried to describe the sensations taking place inside of me. If my joy was great, hers was greater.

"She told me that she had been pouring out her feelings to God. She told Him how she felt such a burden on all of us and how desperately she wanted to offer something in return for the new life she had found through us. She prayed not for herself but that God would somehow relieve my pain. In her wildest dreams she had not hoped for what actually took place. But her deep emotional feeling, apparently lifted me up to freedom.

"When the whirling sensation had abated, we both thanked God for this perfection that was now working out in all things and I *stood up*. That sounds like a small thing but for me it had become a slow and painful exercise in discipline. Not this time. I stood up effortlessly, every joint moving on its cushion of air. I experimented. I bent down. Flexed muscles that had been idle for days because the joints to which they were tied had become immovable. The baby toddled to me, expecting me to pat her head as she hugged my legs, for it had been a long time since I could lean down to cuddle her.

"Now, I leaned down, snatched her up and danced around the room. She chortled with surprise and glee. There is simply no way to describe such sudden freedom, the release that comes after being imprisoned within one's own body.

"I tell myself that there must be some concise sentence that would tie this story all together and end it, but the miracle has not ended. It continues each day."

Take a Moment

- Reflect on the concept of the Perfect Will and how it must flow freely for healing to manifest.

- Is there a conflict that requires you to surrender and remove obstacles that prevent healing to begin?

- Consider the difference between surrendering to the Perfection instead of the illness.

"Not knowing when the dawn will come I
open every door."

— EMILY DICKINSON

CHAPTER 9

Does Toning Always Work?

by Laurel Elizabeth Keyes

THE VOICE RELEASES POWER. Weight lifters release a loud grunt *before* they lift. A karate expert gives a sharp cry *before* striking. Obviously, sound is related to a release of energy. It is a direction of energy in the body.

Until a person has recognized this power of the voice through Toning practice they may not have use of the dynamo at the central station. If one does not speak from the solar center, one is speaking off the top of the head. There is no life in the words. They dip down into the throat area as into a very shallow dish of water and throw it out in a slight spray of scattered droplets. All that is available for speaking is a froth or residue which has been forcibly squeezed out and left over from its source, the body-voice, and it is a dead husk.

Every student will remember sitting through long, dry and

boring lectures given by a professor using this type of voice. Nothing is remembered. Nothing has been given to remember because the professor's mind had no contact with the subconscious mind (feelings), so no new thing was born.

In contrast, there is the speaker who sets the audience afire with enthusiasm and new ideas. Using feeling, the speaker has the power to move others by impregnating the "mother" in the subconscious minds of the audience so that they will give birth to the new ideas.

This is the danger of listening, passively, receptively to impassioned activists. They can hypnotize the minds of their listeners to do what good judgment would deny. Hypnotism is only the process of putting the conscious mind aside and going directly into the subconscious and directing it. One may be standing, wide-eyed and awake, or sitting before a TV screen and be completely hypnotized by the speaker's voice. This is true whether it is experienced directly, or as entertainment. Whatever holds our attention has hold of us. If it reaches our feelings, we are involved, and so we give birth in some area of our life to the ideas which we have let enter our consciousness.

Sound is a motivating force. It appears to be creative or destructive as it collects substance in the wake of its movement, much as water takes on patterns after a motor boat passes through it.

To give you a better idea of this, watch the process of releasing sound in your own body. When you have been quiet, eyes closed and very relaxed for a while, think of speaking. Watch the feeling of tightening, or gathering, which takes place in the solar plexus. Your intention to speak stirs there and you will become aware of the energy coming up into the throat and mouth, and producing sound. At least that is how it should be, and will be, when you have practiced Toning for a while. It is the *alive* voice, the mother-voice which gives form and birth to the idea in the mind.

Remember that the subconscious mind is fascinated by its voice. We hypnotize ourselves daily with repetitious words.

"I am afraid it is going to storm." "I am afraid they won't come." "I am afraid it won't work out." That person is self-conditioned to be afraid—in time, of everything.

Or, the one who says, "I can't stand cold weather." "I can't stand old people." "I can't stand waiting." Soon, a skiing accident has put a leg in a cast, or arthritic knees prevent standing, or a sprained ankle will relieve the person from standing.

The subconscious mind will follow the instructions given to it, with feeling. It is a sensitive computer. It will feed back what has been programmed into it.

When one has been Toning and feels that the subconscious mind is cooperative, one must be careful of the use of the voice for that very reason. "My word shall not return unto me void."

Some amusing incidents came to me when I began Toning. Unconsciously I used the creative formula of "visualization, feeling and breathing." (Breath here refers to that quick intake, or gasp, that carries the image to the subconscious as a camera shutter lets light onto the film and imprints the negative.)

At a lecture I met an acquaintance and noticed the beautiful amethyst stone in a ring which held her neckerchief. It was beautiful (visualization) and I *felt* a kinship with it, for it is my birthstone, and I gasped with delight, "What a beautiful stone. Where did you get it?" I felt I would like to have one like it.

She told me that she had found the ring in Mexico and liked it because it was her birthstone, too. Then I forgot about it.

Later that night, as we drove home, she rather reluctantly drew the ring off and handed it to me. "I feel that this should belong to you."

I protested, but she insisted that she could get another one when she went to Mexico again.

That ring, dear to me, is a constant reminder to keep my mouth shut. Or at least, when I open it to do so with forethought.

A girl who found Toning very easy and a natural thing to do shared some of her early experiences. One day she went to a shop and saw a beautiful suit which she desired intensely. Her nature was impulsive and her purse impoverished. The price of the suit was $110 and she could not afford $10 at that moment. But, she "breathed it in" with deep longing. And went home.

Not too long after that she phoned me. "It works! You know what? I've got three suits. One came from a relative who outgrew it, another came from a friend who wanted to trade it for some babysitting and the other came to me from the people who moved out of the house across the street. They asked me to take their discards to the Goodwill after I'd taken out anything I could use. And in that stuff was a suit, the same color and made almost the same way as the one I saw in the store. Now, how do I stop this suit thing? I don't want any more. I want a new washer and dryer."

I do suggest that people be fully aware of their desires. A married man who begins to Tone should not look at a beautiful young girl and gasp. He may be paying alimony to three or four in no time at all. And the doting, possessive older woman should not look at a small baby and wish that her own children were "little again." Some of her grown children may suddenly leave their brood with her to raise while they go off to find themselves.

The warning must be reiterated. Be sure that you know what you want, because you are almost sure to get it. It may be delayed. That which you desire at twenty-six may not arrive until you are fifty-six, when it can be a burden, but it will come. You are operating a natural law, as reliable as gravity. Be certain that you can handle it wisely. You can no longer hide under ignorance and blame other people for what occurs in your life. You realize that you create your own world and environment. You make the choice to direct your life forces, or you make the choice not to (this invites other people to use your life), but it is still your choice.

I have been asked, "Does Toning never fail?"

In some cases where we have Toned for others, the expected results have not manifested. Here again, none of us is wise enough to direct another's life beyond that one's own will. (Nor should anyone wish to, knowing the results!)

Whenever a person has Toned for him or herself there have always been beneficial changes noticed.

Some people who asked for help had psychological reasons for holding on to their illness, like the woman who used her heart attacks as power over her husband or the lonely woman who perceived that her only opportunity to receive male attention was to keep her allergies and visit her doctor regularly for shots. Then there was the very old man who lay in a coma for months (until his insurance ran out) and was fed by artificial means and given blood transfusions. In such instances we see each person in perfection and feel that the love sent out with the Tone will be of some use at some time. And the act of Toning is always advantageous to the Toner!

Outside of miraculous healings, some conditions are of too long standing for total correction, but Toning can help. A lovely young woman with multiple sclerosis, confined to a wheelchair, told me that she received treatments every four hours and they were very exhausting and painful to her. But when she found out about groaning, they became endurable. "And it sounds so silly that I can't help laughing, and that is the best of all."

Recently, in a hospital wing where terminal cancer patients are cared for I heard a nurse urging her patient to groan. "Don't hold it in," she said gently. "Go ahead and groan, it will be good for you." How pleased I was to know that this is being recognized as one of nature's reliefs.

Then there is the supposition offered, "Well, if you can Tone and correct every ailment, you could go on living indefinitely."

Most of us know that in living there is also the wish to die. Psychiatrists have long tried to deal with that unconscious "death-wish" in patients. Even doctors, who often die of the very illness they were noted for curing in their patients, and spiritual healers, carry a growing desire to be free of their work—of the demands made upon them by people, of trying to meet ever increasing needs of others. There is a longing to rest—a deep, powerful urge to escape all that is expected of one. Death is the only real escape that the subconscious mind understands.

It is as though the divine part of the human being wishes to go on serving unselfishly forever but the body part, the part that is doing the work, becomes exceedingly weary and wishes to rest in the normal cycle of rest experienced in nature.

The many frustrations, disappointments, and even boredom of meeting the same circumstances over and over, accumulate until they become a load too heavy to carry.

If you do not believe this, just imagine that you had to live right here forever! Looking at the same face in the mirror for eternity? Brushing those same teeth, or the same dentures? Having to be fitted with glasses, stumbling over the split vision of bifocals and forever losing your glasses and not being able to find a number in the telephone book or read something handed to you until you could find them? Coping with the ever increasing Christmas card list, and the "numbers system" (telephone numbers, license numbers, zip codes), more and more things to remember? Having to entertain the same people socially, or in business, and eating the same foods, laughing at the same tired jokes? Living with the same set of relatives forever? Even to have to live with yourself, with your own weaknesses, inadequacies, and faults? You think you aren't secretly longing for the time you can escape all that, and rest?

So while it should be possible to extend one's life time considerably with Toning, no one really wants to live in this realm of pain, taxes, noise, hurry and problems forever. But Toning can, without doubt, make the living here much more pleasant, healthier and useful for as long as one does remain in a physical body. And it can help in the transition when it comes.

A beautiful example of that came to me when a mother of three teenage children called me from the hospital. She was there for open-heart surgery. She told me that she had suffered numerous heart attacks and the doctors said that this was the only hope, "but they can't assure me it will be all right. It's a gamble that I must take. I don't mind for myself but I am so afraid to leave my children. What will happen to them?" And she sobbed, "I'm so afraid."

I put everything aside and went into my little sanctuary to Tone for her. It seemed that there would be little hope for a recovery but there could be comfort. It was a beautiful Toning session and I felt at peace afterwards.

The next day she phoned again. Her voice was calm and beautiful, actually it sounded joyous. "I wanted you to know—it's all right. Yesterday, after I talked with you, I had the most wonderful spiritual experience. I was taken right into Heaven. It was so beautiful—so wonderful—the light and peace—there is nothing like it on earth. I didn't even want to come back here! And I knew that my children were in God's keeping which is wiser and more loving than mine. There is nothing to be worried about. Whatever happens Monday [the day of surgery] doesn't matter to me, now. If it took this suffering and illness to bring me to that blessed experience yesterday, it has all been worth it." She thanked me and gave me her blessing.

On Monday the operation was performed but she never regained consciousness. When I attended her funeral I could feel only a sense of the joyousness she had shared with me. It was as though she were saying, "Don't grieve for me, you people. It is for you who don't know the glory that is possible that I grieve."

A year later I saw her children again. While they may have caused their mother concern while she was here, her influence upon them since death was very marked. They spoke of her with such tender affection and admitted that her presence seemed to be with them all the time.

We may not understand the intricate and mysterious weaving of the patterns in life and death, but we do know that in such instances there can be a state of great peace. Toning always helps.

Take a Moment

- Consider how the subconscious mind can be influenced and motivated by your voice.

"Healing is a matter of time, but it is sometimes also a matter of opportunity."

— HIPPOCRATES

CHAPTER 10

Breathing for Sleep

by Laurel Elizabeth Keyes

ALL ASPECTS OF TONING are related to the breath. Breath is life. When we become aware of our breathing patterns we can cooperate with the natural rhythms and have better control of our life.

An important aspect of good health—physical, mental and emotional—is the ability to sleep. Yet it seems that people are finding it increasingly difficult to do this very natural thing because of the pressures and tensions they encounter in daily living.

By changing the breathing pattern it is possible to put oneself to sleep in a matter of minutes.

Many studies are being made of the sleep process. Dr. Nagandra Das, in his research in the subject at the University of Michigan, concluded that the usual procedure of going to sleep requires about an hour of quieting the beta brain waves (rapid thinking activity) down through alpha, theta to delta (deep sleep). It is in delta that the body and mind are restored, so the second hour of sleep is considered the most important. If one retires at 10 P.M., the revitalizing period will be from 11 to midnight, or 11 P.M. to 1 A.M. After that, dream activities increase and release many of the sense-perceptions which have registered on the brain, usually during the previous twenty-four-hour period.

"The dream mechanism is like shaking the day's dust and trash from the rug," Dr. Das told me. "If the mass of information and sensations that flood in on the brain were not allowed to escape through dreams, the burden would cause serious psychological complications." He considered only a small percentage to be psychologically significant, however.

> People try to find meaning in every dream. That is like trying to find jewels in the vacuum sweeper's accumulations. Most dreams are a feedback of the day's registry. Especially those that reflect the TV programs that we watch. People sit before the TV in a passive state, similar to light hypnosis, and the impressions taken in must find an outlet either through dreams or influencing the conscious state. I have seen some people so fascinated by their dreams that they become dream-addicts, waking up several times during the night to record their dreams.

That can be detrimental, in my opinion. It is disturbing their needed rest. The mind is busy enough in waking hours, we should not let it dominate our sleeping, too. If the subconscious has an important message it will come through a vivid dream but that type is rare and cannot be ignored.

Since a third of our lives is spent in sleep, and it is so necessary to our well-being, we should not take it for granted, or as something to do when we have exhausted other interests.

Sleep should be approached with respect, with anticipation and, because it is a mystery, perhaps with awe. Certainly we should prepare for it and have the same delighted expectancy for it as we do for a fine meal. It is nourishment of a different kind.

Many people consider reading in bed an invitation to sleep. Some doctors question that. The awkward position of propping the head up with pillows causes strain on the back and neck as well as eyes. It seems to me to read before going to sleep is like snacking before going out to a banquet. It is filling the mind with more activity. One should be hungry for sleep, and go to it eagerly as to a feast.

It is essential that the body be relaxed, and any method that one finds helpful should be used. However, the secret of sleep is in the breathing rhythm.

Listen to the breathing of a baby or someone asleep. They take in little *short breaths with long pauses in between.*

Oxygen is necessary for brain functioning. We work, speak, think and act on the supply of oxygen in the brain.

WAKING BREATH PATTERN:

When we exhale, we inhale again immediately and so keep the steady flow of oxygen to the brain. When one is hurrying or climbing, the breathing is faster. When one is lifting something, the breath is held for greater strength. Where ventilation is lacking, one becomes drowsy.

It follows that the sleeping breath pattern is just the opposite. Oxygen supply is diminished. We cannot think without it, so the brain becomes quiet and we slip into sleep.

SLEEPING BREATH PATTERN:

Visualization and feeling accompany the change in breath rhythm.

Visualize yourself in a white cloud, or fog. You can see nothing but the soft whiteness around you. You hear nothing. (If there is some noise as there is in any city dwelling, feel that it is receding and will be shut out by the fog.)

Make every breath a sigh. Let go—tensions, thoughts, breathe them *out.* Begin with large sighs and as you release the breath feel yourself slipping comfortably deeper and deeper into this downy cloud where you float like incense on still air.

At first there may be a feeling of wanting to breathe rapidly. Breathe as often as you wish *but keep the air out. Exhale immediately after inhaling.* If there is any idea to keep in mind it is REST. When you exhale say to yourself, "I can breathe as often as I like but I'm too tired—tired—I want to rest. I'll just take a little breath and then rest." Inhale, exhale and enjoy the long pause— you are resting.

Let the sighs be audible at first—empty the lungs with little groans. The pauses between breaths become longer and the breathing more shallow. The brain receives less oxygen, the body is relaxed and deep sleep is the natural result.

It has been claimed that if one will keep the mind fixed on the protecting cloud (keeping all thoughts and pictures outside of it) and the feelings upon rest, and use that rhythm of breathing, one cannot stay awake longer than fifteen minutes. I have found it true in helping many people go to sleep and for myself I know that even after an exciting evening, stimulated by an audience or lecture, I can put myself into deep and refreshing delta-sleep within minutes. I have never taken a sleeping pill, and if you use this technique I believe you will not feel the need for one either.

Here again we are directing the mind to cooperate with the body's natural functioning. Instead of letting it race about wildly, dragging our attention through mazes of unimportant picture-making, we use it to give the body its rightful restoration.

Take a Moment

• Consider this vitalizing daily breathing exercise.

• Close your eyes and send a mental "eeeeee" sound to a radiant sun. Relax and notice the power of six imagined exhalations of the "eeeeee."

"A mortal lives not through that breath that flows in and that flows out. The source of life is another and this causes the breath to flow"

— PARACELSUS

CHAPTER 11

Echo

by Laurel Elizabeth Keyes

"**FROM THE GREAT WHIRL** of Light a spark danced off and in its dance gathered stardust into form. But the spark was fragmented into pieces of the form and lost its way. And, ever seeks return."

You are a spark. Each of us is a spark.

All of us know from experience that we are happiest when we are serving, feeling useful, doing something worthwhile, releasing that inner fire, or spark, into creative form, letting it find its way back to its natural state.

But, we forget and become lost in the objects of our creation.

By nature we are egocentric. The world revolves around "me." Somewhere we lost the understanding that it was we who created our private world—by our desires, evaluations, reactions and aspirations. We behave as a sun which comes to look upon its planets for its source of fuel and light, instead of releasing the energy within itself. We look to the world outside for the answers which should come from within.

We expect atomic weapons to be our strength. We look for something outside—a faraway divine power, the government, laws or organizations, to protect and provide for us and do what we should feel capable of doing for ourselves. All these things have a place, but they become detrimental to us if we depend entirely upon such sources and forget to develop our own enormous potentialities.

Power comes from concentrated forces. Sunlight falls upon a sheet of paper and nothing happens, but when the rays of the sun are focused through a magnifying glass, the paper begins to burn. The laser beam is our recognition and use of such power.

With an understanding of bringing together and focusing the forces within us, through Toning, we can direct these energies to the achievement of which we are capable. We, too, can catch on fire and burn—we can expand that spark, which became so coated and crystallized in its fragmented state, to reunite with its Source.

It is possible to be creative, to change our environment, to be healed, to make life useful and, most of all, joyous. Proper use of the voice is a means of directing the forces in our field to unite with their perfect pattern so that we may function in its harmony and be as wonderful as we ARE. We are the only creatures capable of changing our lives through imagination and will. It is our divine inheritance and we should claim it.

You can create a new world for yourself through the power of your voice.

Let your life sing!

Take a Moment

- Creativity starts with a spark to change. Consider the changes you would like to see in your life.

- Reflect on how your voice can direct the energy it takes to move forward.

"The human voice is the organ of the soul"

– HENRY WADSWORTH LONGFELLOW

CHAPTER 12

Toning and Prayer

by Laurel Elizabeth Keyes (Postscript, 1976)

OFTEN PEOPLE HAVE ASKED if I consider audible prayer to be more powerful than silent prayer. The intensity of feeling has much to do with the efficacy of any wish, but it appears that sound has a definite influence.

There is a story from India that points this out. "If a person in the room wishes me to bring a glass of water and silently requests it, I may not receive the message, but if he speaks aloud I shall respond immediately."

"But, God is not deaf," it was argued.

"Ah, but God is very busy and if I speak aloud, someone is bound to hear and come to my aid."

Sound does set many forces into motion. In a recent paper by Dr. William Tiller[10] he writes, "If we compare magnetoelectric light (ME) with electromagnetic light (EM) then for the same wavelength the ME light has a frequency ten orders of magnitude larger than EM light."

It seems reasonable that sound, as light, has subtle frequencies, perhaps not yet recognized, which in the same way are of larger magnitude than previously understood, and it is on them that Toning travels from person to person across space. We may not understand how—but we do know that results are evidenced when Toning is practiced. We stand in the humorous position of the young person who brought some new evidence to a scientific Board for review. A rigid old scientist said, "Young woman, if you were educated as we are you would realize that what you have done is impossible!"

We know that fine sand on a drum takes geometric patterns if the drum is placed on a piano which is being played. Sound moves matter.

Recently a grant was given for scientific study of the influence, if any, of silent mental "treatment" on live tissue. The experiments were conducted by a scientist in the research laboratory of a Colorado university, under the usual strict controlled conditions. Practitioners of different faiths attempted to increase cell growth with their various methods. To date, none have had any influence upon the cells. (However, it must be remembered that this experiment was made upon cells taken from living tissue, placed in plastic dishes in an incubator in a laboratory, and were not connected with the consciousness of a living body which might respond in a different manner. There have been many cases of healings reported by such methods so they cannot be discounted.)

Interestingly enough, when sound was introduced to absent treatment, cells *were* influenced. A small group of people using Toning and chanting, along with visualization and feeling, caused the cell growth in the plastic dishes to increase 13 percent. This group was twenty-five miles from the laboratory, so it was not sound as we hear it that reached the cells.

When I was given the opportunity to try the experiment I decided to destroy malignant cells taken from a brain tumor. I Toned for five minutes, twice a day for three days, visualizing the cells changing into light, vanishing. Instead of dying—they grew 6 percent! That convinced me that "life cannot be destroyed. It changes form or expands in its own pattern." By directing my attention and voice to the cells, I was watering the weeds, and *they grew in their own pattern* which was malignancy. It appears that consciousness focused upon living substance stimulates it as sunlight upon a plant. Could this be part of the reason that in spite of billions of dollars spent on cancer research, the disease increases each year? that so much attention placed upon it is feeding it?

On my next attempt to influence the cells in their plastic dishes, miles away, I Toned for five minutes, twice a day for three days, visualizing their expansion and Toning with a feeling of great joyousness. There was a 17 percent increase in growth. Granted, that is small, but it is evidence that sound produced by the human voice can influence cell growth, miles away. Think what it can do to the cells of our body as we speak or Tone!

From this it seems obvious that to treat disease we should not focus attention and feeling upon it, but visualize and Tone for the healthy, normal cells and let them displace the foreign ones as they become more vigorous and grow in their perfect pattern.

"Speak the word only, and my servant shall be healed," as given in Matthew 8:8, takes on new meaning when we realize that the voice is a vehicle for good, or destruction, as we release its power.

Chants and mantras, as well as prayers, grew out of the human response to release feelings of adoration, worship or supplication. Dr. Judith Tyberg writes in her book *The Language of the Gods*:

> Primitive language was born from imitating sounds of nature and from vocal expressions responding to physical and vital movements innate with their own essential sound-vibrations. Every sound in Sanskrit is said to have two aspects, the more audible sound and the subtler essential sound-element behind, vibrant with the meaning natural to it. This vibrant sense-sound within is the real or fundamental sound, called *sphota*.

The outward audible sound, its instrument of expression, is called the external sound. The *sphota* arises in the indivisible, permanent Spirit, and is eternally luminous with power and when the spoken word, its vehicle, is perfectly sounded within and without, it stimulates this inner vibrant activity with the result that the power within responds and illuminates.[11]

Performed with this understanding, chants can be very effective. Familiar ones are *Om, Om Mani Padmi Hum,* and *So-Ham.* From Christian origins we have, *Lord, have mercy upon me, Praise the Lord* and *Halleluia,* among others. *Nam Myoho Renge Kyo,* introduced in Japan in the thirteenth century, is used today in many countries. The Fransisters studied the chants of many religions and found certain rhythms and sounds (such as the "O," "mmm" and "ho") common to most, so they devised one that can be chanted on a chord or to a favorite melody. *One with all life, Holy I am.* It is good to chant as one is doing physical work, driving a car, working in rhythm with machinery, almost anywhere and any time. It can be done softly, almost whispered, so long as one is hearing it inwardly. It keeps the mind occupied with the beauty of sound and permits the soul to be free in its communion with its Source.

"I will sing with the spirit, and I will sing with the understanding also."[12]

Since the first experiments with Toning in 1957, examples of benefits continue to increase. Even I am astonished at some of the results related to me. The greatest, of course, are felt when one Tones for oneself.

Toning energizes us and gives us confidence that we can control our lives. While we live in a rapidly changing world and are confronted with circumstances not always to our liking, Toning gives us the feeling that we have full authority over our *reactions* to those circumstances.

We can always BE the person we wish to be as long as we are conscious of the creative power within, and attune ourselves to our divine pattern through the practice of Toning.

Take a Moment

• Consider a prayer, chant, mantra, or song that resonates with your inner soul and clearly expresses your purpose in life.

• Reflect on the sounds of these words as you speak or sing them out loud.

"A truly creative person rids him or herself of all self-imposed limitations"

— GERALD JAMPOLSKY

Toning

PART II

CHAPTER 13

A New Century of Tone:
Research, Review and Potential
by Don Campbell

IT IS EXCITING to bring "toning" up to date in this new, revised edition of Laurel Keyes' book. There have been many questions raised about the voice and its powers since the book was written thirty-five years ago. There have been a dozen popular books about intuitive toning; they followed publication of my book *The Roar of Silence* in 1999.

Joy Gardner-Gordon, Jonathan Goldman, Dick Rigby and Susan Hale have used tone as a fundamental tool in their work and writings. Over a dozen graduate students have prepared major papers for degrees in nursing, psychology and music therapy that have deepened our understanding of Toning. The research and writings of Peggy Deak, James Markham, Beverly Pierce and Diane Eisenman have inspired me. They have truly enhanced the understanding of what the rigor of Toning can do to assist in health. They have questioned some of the convenient myths of instant health and probed into the deeper influences of sound on posture, skin temperature, childbirth and trauma.

As I have reviewed the notes of the sixteen mentors and the hundreds of students at the Institute for Music Health and Education (1988 through 1997) and the nine "Therapeutic Sound School" yearlong programs throughout the United States, I have found many interesting threads that weave the mystery of tone together.

One of the most constant stories that has been recorded about tone concerns its power to reduce pain and discomfort. From broken limbs to severe migraine headaches, Toning seems to bring immediate relief and divert attention from the pain to the breath. The most natural responses to pain are the passive moans and groans as well as the active "ooouch" or "eikes". Naturally, we often hear the four-letter mantras that are an instant reaction to pain, but they seldom elongate any positive effect. I suspect they just enhance the pain, aggravation and inconvenience.

I have defined tone as "the elongation of a sound using the breath and voice no matter the quality or pitch of the sound." Music Therapist Kenneth Bruscia defines toning as "the use of vocal sounds to restore vibratory patterns of the body within a perfect electro-magnetic field, thereby enabling the body and all of its parts to function in harmony." As Laurel Keyes said earlier in this book, "Toning is the freeing and releasing of the body-voice unhindered by the mind."

Tone can also be defined as pitch, as in "singing a high tone." It can also describe how bright or dark a sound is. In physiology, tone designates the normal tension or resistance to stretch a healthy muscle.

Dr. Alfred Tomatis hinted at the importance of elongated vowel sounds in the form of Gregorian chant. The long melismatic lines of tones, he suggests, have dynamic effects on the mind and body. As an MD, Tomatis was called to a monastery in the south of France in the late 1960's where all the monks had become fatigued, listless and somewhat depressed. It was after Vatican II. Reforms had been made to the duties, diets and more precisely, the daily prayers which were sung in Latin. The long, lovely, mellow lines were replaced by simple text and a folk song accompaniment.

Tomatis declared that the cause of the despondent state of bodies and spirits was not physiological, but audiological. He concluded that by simply singing they had stopped charging their brains and were no longer empowering their minds and spirits with the charged sounds of vowels. After a short time of restoring their prayers and meditation times with Gregorian chant, their health, spirits and work improved. A detailed description of these events is recorded in my book *Music, Physician for Times to Come*.

Music Therapist Mark Rider, Ph.D., became interested in Toning after reading about Dr. Tomatis's research in how acoustic sound affects stress. In Rider's 1997 book *The Rhythmic Language of Health and Disease,* he states:

I have experimentally studied the effects of toning on the human body by having subjects vocalize on a syllable and pitch of their choice for ten minutes. This type of toning seems to provide subjects with a continuous high frequency stimulation from the harmonics of the tone, perhaps chosen intuitively based on the subconscious perception of high frequency hearing loss. If so, this procedure would constitute a natural form of biofeedback. When compared to singing familiar songs, we found that the toning condition elicited a significantly higher immune system response (sIgA) and a lower heart rate than the singing condition. The toning condition also elicited the lowest post-test measures of confusion, suggesting that some enhancement of brainwave activity may have occurred. One researcher has discussed the possibility that chanting influences the vibration of cerebrospinal fluid in the ventricles of the brain (Bentov). Furthermore, certain resonance patterns created by the chanting purportedly enhance psycho-spiritual communication abilities.

Whether one is chanting or Toning, the breathing becomes deeper and longer over a period of minutes. This enhances the relaxation response as long as it is comfortable to make the sounds and the jaw is relaxed. It becomes very difficult to tone if there is stress or fear in the mind. A short phrase becomes longer as states of tension are released.

The very basic urge to tone is innate within us. Humming and cooing are associated with an infant's pleasurable sensations. It is heard when being fed and when there is satisfaction. In this early oral phase, the tone is associated with comfort and safety. Also, this is the time when the mother may hum or gently sing lullabies to relax and soothe the infant. The earliest sounds are made in the back of the throat; as the baby begins to gain control of its tongue, the sounds change and become more varied. The tones change with babbling, the appearance of teeth and physical movement. It is also quite obvious to every parent that the variety of vowels of their newborns all have different meanings, from joy to pain to frustration or hunger.

When we return to some of these early sounds, we can easily tap into the joy and perhaps pain of the early oral phase of life. I noticed that approximately one in twenty Toning students would mention "becoming like a baby" when they were Toning an "ooou" or "hum" sound.

It is quite obvious that what goes into the ear comes out the mouth. Our language—its accents and dialects—is made by the tones and the phonemes that give form and rhythm to the vowels. Yet, we often inhibit our most natural sound making. Paul Moses, MD, states in his remarkable book *The Voice of Neurosis* that our linguistic vocal range has become smaller and smaller throughout history, so much so that we are at a point where "the spectrum of speech range is now merely reflective of a small emotional scale on which our rational articulation plays."

Each culture uses only a small part of its vocal potential. Some American Indian, African and Asian languages are quite muscular in character. The throat singing technique of the Mongolians and Tibetans is husky, rich in overtones in contrast to some Eurasian languages that are high and delivered with more tension in the voice.

Toning creates a physical and non-mental place where all languages unite and blend the place of base emotions with exhalation and at times expression. Whether one is an elementary school teacher bringing out a shy student's communication skills through musical games or a psychiatrist assisting a patient's release of trauma or abuse, the powers of Toning are fundamental for relaxing the mind and body.

At the Institute for Music, Health and Education, exploration of the Toning voice went far beyond the normal spontaneous experiences mentioned in this book. Three courses were developed for the adventurous and disciplined student:

The Healing Aspects of Tone and Voice
The Healing Aspects of Tone and Color
Analysis of the Voice and Self-generated Tonal Applications

Variations of each course took up to nine months depending on the daily rigor of the student. It was suggested that ten to fifteen minutes of Toning be done on a daily basis. Each of the Toning sessions was tape-recorded, with a simple tone, then a glissando at the beginning. Then the Toning continued without being recorded, and then another tonal glissando was made on tape. It was possible for the mentor to hear the difference the Toning made on the speaking voice and the vocal range as demonstrated in the glissando. (A glissando is a gliding sound on a vowel tone from the lowest to the highest sound in a voice without any stress. In other words, sliding from the lowest sound to the most easily reached high sound. The same experience can be observed from the highest point in the voice gliding down to the lowest.)

Each day in the Institute's Toning program suggested experiments in different postures. Some days there was movement, on others one would be quietly sitting. Sometimes eyes were open and at other times, eyes were closed. Frequently the student would lay down comfortably on the floor. Over a period of months, the voice began to open. In a meditation-like state, the tone would simply rest in the voice with no effort whatsoever. It was also predictable that one or two of the vowel sounds would periodically be blocked and uncomfortable. The cause could be physical, emotional or mental.

The goal of this program was to open the ear and the voice in order to allow the ease and flow of the sound to become natural and unencumbered. It was always interesting to observe professional vocalists who found most of the exercises quite difficult at the beginning. They had to surrender to a vocal state where there was no performance or outer concern about the beauty of their sound.

It was noted in this program that the ear slightly changed in its ability to focus on certain frequencies. Using the guidelines of the Tomatis Audiological Listening Test, we were able to notice if there were changes in certain ranges of auditory perception in bone and air conduction after three to six months of Toning. Never were there dynamic changes in hearing abilities, but the general richness of the voice often improved and small dips in perception of specific frequencies were no longer noticed.

In the advanced courses, we experimented with color and sound. By observing what colors came to mind with different tones and hearing what tones were spontaneously produced after looking at colors, we found a wide variety of responses. When a color was imagined for a week, it would change daily with some students and be constant with others. When the eyes were focused on a color card for ten minutes, it might start on one vowel sound and proceed to two or three others over the session. The copious notes from these sessions are quite interesting and provided the conclusion that every person is influenced by colors in a different tonal manner. That any note would correspond to a color was never spontaneously noted. It solely depended on the range of the individual voice and the comfort zone of tonal production.

In general, Toning created five basic experiences for the students: Excitation, Relaxation, Boredom, Catharsis and Altered States of Consciousness. The ease in which each student began the course allowed a very gradual unfoldment of blocked mental and physical energies. We never encouraged long sessions with tone because of the induction of catharsis and altered states. Generally the rule was to tone as long as it felt natural and easy. In the beginning stages, that would often be just two to three minutes at a time. Then after resting for a couple of minutes, it could be resumed. For the student who could only do it for a few minutes a day, it would slowly increase by a minute or two per week and top off at ten minutes. To push the voice beyond its natural flow could easily cause catharsis or altered states. This was never encouraged without a therapist or experienced guide. In all, the Toning experience was always safe and exploratory.

The stories in the next chapter reflect the variety of experiences within the first few weeks of Toning. In the closing chapter and on the CD that accompanies this book, there will be some easy Toning exercises for you to explore the powers of your own voice.

CHAPTER 14

Stories from the Voice

by Don Campbell

FOR THE PAST TWENTY YEARS, I have heard of miracles in the mind, body and heart through Toning. I always think the miracle was just ready to happen and the tone just gave a little energy and triggered a flow to a great moment of healing. Without making unrealistic claims, I do think the power of transformation is always ready to happen.

I have selected a dozen experiences that I find of interest that may inspire you to develop your own program. I have used many words that have a prolonged vowel sound to help the image, the meaning and the ease of Toning. "Peace," "Joy," "All," "Love" and "Now" each have different tonal energies and are easy to produce for ten to fifteen minutes.

Many physical and mental conditions can find benefit through Toning. It is a constant and useful tool used for pain reduction. It helps divert the mind and oxygenize the body. Toning helps balance the brainwaves and usually raises the skin and body temperature. Later in this book, I will give you a five-day plan to help you open your vocal energies.

Here are firsthand accounts of the beginning stages of tonal experiences that may inspire you to be creative and patient as you begin to Tone.

Hum

I began my first days of Toning with a meditation focus from *The Roar of Silence.* I hummed with a relaxed jaw for ten minutes and kept my mind focused on the thought of "The All in every sound."

The experience was very soothing. When I started humming my dog stopped playing and immediately lay down to nap. Shortly after I was done she got up. I felt like someone was with me when I hummed. This was an easy and peaceful experience. I made a very comfortable transition into silence afterwards. Later I started to hum some songs I used to sing with my family as a child. The Toning opened up wonderful musical memories that had been asleep in me for twenty years.   – JOHN, age 27

Hum Ah

This is the fourth day of humming. It was very powerful today. I felt great sadness for "little me." Tears flowed. At one point the pitch went to a higher note and a release occurred which had that "breath of fresh air" feeling about it.

Later that day, I had a massage and decided to try to tone at the beginning of the session. I started on *Ah* and let vowels come as they would. I was aware of great heat moving throughout my body. It was very quiet and the tones were short since I was lying on my stomach. I imagined sending the tone to the area of my body where I was being touched.

After a month, I am astonished to see how these innocently done Toning exercises have added up to pages of detailed information about my inner experiences and physical sensations. The voice is a map of the body; it has characteristics as particular and peculiar as a fingerprint. The voice is a truth-telling instrument. How much of my truth am I willing to know, grow, and express? Toning has changed my life.　　　　　　　　　　　– GRACE, age 35

Hum

The hum exercise brought a great amount of energy into my body. At different times, I felt the *Hum* moved into and through areas of tension in a cleansing manner. My organs felt vitalized and balanced. As more energy poured in with the vibrating *Hum,* I became a circular column of soft light. A sense of peace and wholeness filled me.   – ALEXANDRA, age 23

Hah

Bringing my awareness to my breath and watching my inhalation and exhalation was comfortable. When I moved my awareness to my heart, I felt uncomfortable. As Don put it, my songbody began to go unconscious. I needed a reminder of where to focus, so I put a hand upon my heart. This physical reminder helped. I began to visualize a spark of life force with the *Hah* with each heartbeat. I had a hard time putting the visual image and the sound together.

Suddenly on the third day of this week, I sensed a brownish cloud around me, full of pain and sadness. The *Hah* and the heartbeats had to move around the sadness. I stayed with this feeling for ten long, long minutes in my heart area and felt an energy block. The sound was quiet and not forced. Then suddenly a new pattern emerged. My mind became acutely active. Thoughts arose and I became distracted, losing my focus on my heart. Tension in my chest dissipated. At this point, I ended the Toning meditation. I realize I have some sadness in myself and this will help me slowly embrace and release it.

– JOYCE, age 41

Ah

The *Ah* sound is very relaxing. This meditation sound is easy for me to focus on. I found as I reviewed the past twenty-four hours, my *Ahs* switched to a soft, gentle tone to a radiant, full voiced expression of pleasure. It was like I started with a yawning sound and resulted in a wonderful sense of active participation in life.   – JOYCE, age 41

Who

When I started this exercise, I stood up and felt calm in a quiet still point. I was quiet for a minute or two before I made a sound. Then when I made the *Who* or *Hu* sound I instantly had all of this passionate, explosive energy. I felt hot and was burning with energy and did not know what to do. I realized I could not stuff away this exciting and good energy anymore. I had hit a point of real joy and power. The tone moved up and down, around my whole body. I found I did not want to go high. I saw a translucent, shimmering beam of light moving within me. The feelings were positive and peacefulness always was present.

On completion of this workshop, I immediately noticed an increase in my body awareness. Both body and voice, now activated and stimulated, were determined to continue their journey of self-exploration. I found myself enjoying contact with others in a new, refreshing approach that felt truly authentic and more loving.

By understanding my own space (internal and external) and its needs, I became acutely sensitive to others' needs as well, and I began to experience a level of interaction that felt appropriate, safe, and supportive for everyone concerned. It was a sense of freedom, a bodily felt freedom, which I believe is a key for integration in my work with others as a therapist.   – KEVIN, age 45

Ah

What I felt from experimenting for three days with the *Ah* sound was the perfectness of life. This is very rare for me. I have felt something similar from biking in the mountains. That is more like a high feeling. This was quiet and inward. My heart as it beats is, in itself, a beautiful symphony of rhythms and points of light and dark. I have never had this kind of experience before. I became aware of the depth of my "being." I became one with my heart as the Toning of *Ah* was invoked. This Toning relaxed me, my heart slowed down, and I felt very soothed and warm in this intimate moment.   – SHIRLEY, age 58

Eee

I did the *Eee* meditation twice, because I experienced a state of being in which I felt whole, sufficient and connected—a state of spiritual grace in which I could meet life or death with total acceptance without fear, regret, or loneliness. It is difficult to find sufficient words for this—it seems to be beyond verbal description. I believe that the achievement of this state of acceptance of all life and one's connection to it is the essence of my spiritual journey. I believe acceptance is a way of bringing oneself to the Self, to others, to the world, and to the universal divine truth with clarity, detachment and compassion. It is my way of seeing and understanding without judgment. Acceptance does not, however, imply suppressing one's personal likes, dislikes, and values. Rather, it encompasses and transcends them. The acceptance of myself is a trust that my mental, physical, emotional and spiritual capacities are sufficient and OK and include both my strengths and weaknesses. – SHIRLEY, age 58

Eh

At first, this meditation was a little painful. The "sparks" were pinpricks. The *Eh* sound certainly brought an open feeling to my upper chest and it seemed there was a bit of a push and pull going on. By the third day of the sound, the struggle disappeared. The needlepoint feeling was still there sometimes, but my resistance to opening had gone. I made sure I was in a safe place at a time I would not be disturbed. It seemed essential that I create a space like that; I felt I was really inside my body. This was sometimes comfortable, sometimes not. I was creating my own sonic acupuncture session. I will continue to explore all different vowel sounds and explore the different sensations from each one whether the pitch is high or low. I have learned to keep going for ten or fifteen minutes, then the barriers are released and my mind and body are balanced. — MARIAN, age 50

Movement

I explored the vowels *a, e, i, o, u* with movement. For each vowel I first let it resonate inside of my body and then let it take an improvisational form of movement. I found that in doing the vowels *a, e,* and *i,* my movement wanted to go outward from my center. For the vowels *o* and *u* the energy was directed inward. I found a lot of power while exploring the vowels with movement. I was thinking how helpful it would be to include voice within a dance class and how much deeper the movement would go into the body.

How wonderful that we are moving in the direction of resurrecting the ancient wisdom of Toning. It makes this information and practice seem all the more crucial to our survival and health. — JONATHAN, age 33

Author's note: I suggested to Jonathan the work of Rudolph Steiner, who developed the school of Eurhythmy that focused on the tone of movement.

Hum

As I listened to Don lecture on Toning, I remembered a time when my family was vacationing on a houseboat on Lake Powell. My small son became very ill with a fever and we were hours away from the dock and some medical assistance. I found myself humming to him, lightly and lovingly. While we were waiting for help, I realized I had been humming through instinct for over six hours. It was the most natural sound a concerned mother could make.
— REBA, age 42

CHAPTER 15

Toning–Exercises for Alignment

by Don Campbell

WHETHER YOU HAVE BEEN singing all your life or have never been a vocal person, the following five-day program is for you. Even if you once Toned, this is an ideal way to realign your mind and body for more creative, relaxed and energized activities.

Five days plus five weeks

The five-day sampler will open the vowel sounds to your ears, mouth and body. Then, take just one of the vowels per week and let the inner discovery begin. Prepare a journal that will help you develop your own program in months to come.

Each day, begin by writing about your physical, emotional and mental state. Take a few minutes to simply evaluate without judgment what is going on before you begin Toning. Then take ten to fifteen minutes to Tone and reflect on your experiences.

Before Toning

I notice in my mind:

I observe in my body:

I sense in my emotions:

DATE	TIME OF DAY	VOWEL TONE

After Toning

I noticed in my mind:

I observed in my body:

I sensed in my emotions:

Images or curious experiences I had while Toning today:

TONING DURATION	SPECIFIC IMAGES/EXPERIENCES
_____ MINUTES	

Feel free to use the form on the previous two pages as an outline for your notes. Also, you may photocopy those two pages so you have a good uniform way of remembering your Toning experiences.

The suggestions in these exercises cannot be accessed with the mind. Only the sound carries the power. After decades of Toning, the experience is still new every day, creating an immediate pathway for clarity, release and transformation. It only takes a few minutes to bring me into the awakened place of silence where I can listen to the heart of creation: the breath of God, the stillness of Soul, the place of balance.

On the accompanying CD, Laurel Keyes will introduce you to Toning. I will guide you through the following exercises, so you can hear and feel the power of these elongated vocal sounds.

1. Ready—Set—Hum

When I was researching my book *The Mozart Effect*, I was amazed to find a wonderful letter that Mozart wrote that describes his Toning experience:

> When I am, as it were, completely myself, entirely alone and of good cheer…my ideas flow best and most abundantly. Whence and how they come, I do know not; nor can I force them. Those ideas that please me I retain in memory, and, am accustomed, as I have been told, to hum them to myself.

Do you ever notice yourself humming in the car, shower or bus? Is it always a sign of a good mood, free of thought? Do you ever notice yourself responding to someone's ideas with a questioning short "hum"? When you are in a bakery, do you ever "yum" or "hum" over a pastry? The *Hum* sound has many inflections and meanings. In this exercise, just enjoy the physical sensation of the *Hum* without producing a melody or song.

Close your eyes and put your hands on your cheeks and just begin to *Hum*. Forget about the sound, just notice the feeling of the vibration. Always remember to relax your jaw and let the sound find its relaxed place. You may want to allow your voice to glide up and down a few times, just so you discover your comfort place.

After a few minutes, just relax your hands and enter the place of humming lightly for ten minutes. If you are tired and become bored, just relax in silence for a few breaths and begin again.

Make your notes in your journal before and after Toning.

2. Aaah—OK

The wonderful *Aaah* sound automatically evokes the relaxation response. It is a common sound as we are waking up or going to sleep. It is the most contagious of all sound. Yawn two or three times and the people around you will likely respond by yawning.

This is the ideal sound for the release of tension and stress. As your inhalations become deeper, your body gets the signal that it is time to slow down the brainwaves and bring oxygen into the body.

Open your jaw slightly and let the *Aaah* be released in a short breath. Then slowly increase the length of the breath. It is not necessary to make a loud sound, just a soothing one.

Close your eyes and just rest in the *Aaah* sound for a few minutes.

Then experiment with a more charged *Ah* (as in Ah-HA) sound. It has more energy and is used at times as a reaction to surprise or as a confirming exclamation. Explore the range of the *Aaah* sound. Put your hand gently around your throat and listen to the sound as if you were deaf to the sound and able to hear just through the vibration.

Settle into your own *Aaah* for ten minutes…and enjoy the flow of breath.

3. Eeee

This is the caffeine of all tones. It can awaken your mind and charge your body within a minute. Making the sound too loudly can create a headache and discomfort. It can also serve as a wonderful stimulant to help you stay awake while driving your car.

Begin the *Eeee* sound in a very relaxed state with your lips slightly parted. Start by thinking the word "peace" for two or three minutes as you tone. Rest for a moment and then make the *Eeee* sound in a loud voice for thirty seconds. Remain quiet with closed eyes and notice what you are sensing.

Now return to the calming, relaxed *Eeee* sound for ten minutes.

Never strain the voice. You may wish to stretch, rotate your head gently and move your body if you feel stress within the voice.

There are dozens of great ways to Tone and you will find the best way to open your voice and receive its benefits. In the beginning stages, it is best to sit with the eyes closed and just be "inside" the sound. You may notice colors or images appearing in your mind. Simply observe them and treat them as being curious without any judgment.

4. Oh—OM

The power of the *Oh* and *Om* sound can easily vibrate the body. From the deep, rich sound of the chest to the bright overtones in the head, the *Oh* has been a central sound for meditation and transformation in Eastern and Western religions.

In Hinduism, all was dark and still in the womb of the universe, when the first movement created the *Om* sound. In Bali, a legend tells of a giant gong that when struck created the *OOOOm* sound that became the bridge between the Creator and the created. Japan's Shinto goddess was in full retreat in a cave and there was darkness and no life. At the first sound, she came forward and life began.

Whether it is a Big Bang or a subtle sound that starts after the breath begins, this *Oh* represents the primary act of creation.

"Oh really?" "Oh no!" "Oh OOOh." Your *Oh* can represent wonder, surprise or the deepest doubt. As you begin the sound, release all conceptions of what it should be.

Begin by yawning, stretching your jaw and gliding up and down to find the easiest place to produce the sound. If you continue to explore the *Om* sound for a few days, you can visualize your heart area and allow the sound to radiate from the center of your body. In the first few minutes, just get to know the sound.

This tone is worthy of a lifetime of exploration.

5. Oouu

After days of experimentation, it is time just to enjoy the sweetest and most pleasurable sound.

Oouu is comfortable for the mind and body. Experiment with walking, lying down or sitting with eyes open as you explore the wonder of tone.

Selected References

Andrews, Donald Hatch. *The Symphony of Life,* Lee's Summit, MO, Unity Books, 1966.

Assagioli, Roberto. *Psychosynthesis,* N.Y., Viking Press, 1965.

Bach, Marcus. *The Inner Ecstasy,* Nashville, TN., Abingdon Press, 1969.

Barnett, Lincoln. *The Universe & Dr. Einstein,* New York, Harper Bros., 1948.

Day & DeLaWarr. *Matter in the Making,* London, Vincent Stuart, 1970.

DeBit, Ralph M. *Healing Technic and Clear Thinking,* Denver, CO., Cooper Press, 1946.

DeBit, Ralph M. *Problem of Good & Evil,* Santa Barbara, CA, Rowny Press, 1959.

Green, Elmer. *Biofeedback for Mind-Body Self-Regulation; Healing & Creativity,* Los Altos, CA, Academy of Parapsychology & Medicine, 1971.

Hall, Manly P. *Secret Teachings of All Ages,* Los Angeles, CA, Philosophical Research Society, Inc., 1928.

Heisenberg, Werner. *Physics & Beyond,* New York, Harper & Row, 1971.

Higgins, Godfrey. *Anacalypsis,* New Hyde Park, NY, University Books, 1963.

Hills, Christopher. *Nuclear Evolution,* London. Centre Coin. Pub., 1968.

Jacobi, Jolande. *Psychology of Carl Jung,* New Haven, CT, Yale University Press, 1951.

Kilner, Walter J. *The Human Aura,* New Hyde Park, NY, University Books, 1965.

Kingsland, William. *The Gnosis of Ancient Wisdom in Christian Scriptures,* Wheaton, IL, Theosophical Pub., 1937.

Kuhn, Alvin B. *Lost Key to the Scriptures & Shadow of Third Century,* Wheaton, IL, Theosophical Pub., 1972.

Murchie, Guy. *Music of the Spheres,* NY, Dover Pub., 1967.

Ostrander & Schroeder, *Psychic Discoveries Behind the Iron Curtain,* Englewood Cliffs, NJ, Prentice-Hall, 1970.

Ouspensky, P. K. *The Fourth Way,* NY, Vintage Books, 1957.

Pike, Albert. *Morals & Dogma,* Richmond, VA, Jenkins Pub., 1914.

Tiller, William. *Radionics, Radiesthesia & Physics,* Los Altos, CA, Academy of Parapsychology & Medicine, 1971.

Tompkins, Peter. *Secrets of the Great Pyramid,* NY, Harper & Row, 1971.

Waters, Frank. *The Book of the Hopi,* NY, Viking Books, 1963.

References Updated for New Edition

Campbell, Don. *Creating Inner Harmony: Using Your Voice and Music to Heal,* Hay House, 2007.

Campbell, Don. *Heal Yourself With your Own Voice,* Boulder, CO, Sounds True, 1991.

Campbell, Don. *The Roar of Silence,* Wheaton, IL, Quest Books, 1991.

Campbell, Don & Wilson, Tim. *Healing with Tone and Chant,* Wheaton, IL, Quest Books, 2001.

D'Angelo, James. *The Healing Power of the Human Voice, Mantras, Chants, and Seed Sounds for Health and Harmony,* Rochester, VT, Healing Arts Press, 2000.

Goldman, Jonathan. *Healing Sounds, The Power of Harmonics,* Rockport, MA, Element Inc., 1992.

Goodchild, Chloë. *Your Naked Voice,* Boulder, CO, Sounds True, 2006.

Love, Roger, with Frazier, Donna. *Set Your Voice Free,* Boston, New York, London; Little, Brown, 1999.

Nakkach, Silvia. *Who is Singing? Embracing the Physical and Spiritual Dimension of the Voice,* Emeryville, CA, Vox Mundi, 2008.

Newham, Paul. *The Healing Voice,* Boston, MA, Element Books, Inc., 1999.

Ruland, Heiner, translated by John F. Logan. *Expanding Tonal Awareness,* London, Rudolf Steiner Press, 1992.

Snodgrass, Cynthia. *The Sonic Thread, Sound as a Pathway to Spirituality,* NY, Paraview Press, 2002.

Notes

1. Romans 7:19–19.

2. *Morals and Dogma,* by Albert Pike, 1914, p. 251.

3. *Book of the Hopi,* Frank Waters, Viking Press, 1963.

4. *Morals and Dogma,* Albert Pike, 1914, p. 97.

5. *Sound of Music and Plants,* Dorothy Retallack, DeVorss & Co., 1973.

6. "Radionics, Radiesthesia & Physics," *Varieties of Healing Experience.*
   Dr. William Tiller, Academy of Parapsychology & Medicine,
   Los Altos, CA, 1971.

7. *Colloidal Structure,* Ralph M. DeBit. Rowny Press, Santa Barbara, CA, 1957.

8. "Radionics, Radiesthesia & Physics," p. 58. *Varieties of Healing
   Experience.* Dr. William Tiller, Academy of Parapsychology & Medicine,
   Los Altos, CA, 1971.

9. Ibid.

10. *Positive and Negative Space-Time Frames as Conjugate Systems,*
    Dr. William Tiller, Department of Material Science, Stanford University,
    Stanford, CA, 1975.

11. *Language of the Gods,* Dr. Judith M. Tyberg, East-West Cultural Center,
    Los Angeles, CA, 1967.

12. 1 Corff. 14:15.

LAUREL ELIZABETH KEYES (1907–1983) was a teacher and author in Denver, Colorado. She lectured nationally and taught metaphysical and psychological classes for over thirty years and served as Director of the Restorium, a retreat house in the Colorado mountains. She was the author of many spiritual books and discovered the technique of Toning.

DON CAMPBELL is a recognized authority on the transformative power of music, listening and The Mozart Effect®. He is the author of nine books, including 1997's best-seller, *The Mozart Effect*®. In addition, he has produced 16 albums including the accompanying *Music for The Mozart Effect*® series for adults and children, which dominated the *Billboard* Classical charts in 1998 and 1999. Campbell also is a leading lecturer and consultant to organizations ranging from corporations to parenting groups to symphony orchestras.

For more information on Don Campbell's books and CDs as well as a vast guide to music, music therapy, education, and health:

The Mozart Effect Resource Center
PO Box 800, Boulder, CO 80306

www.mozarteffect.com
(800) 721-2177

Barbara Dalberg, a student of Laurel Keyes, gives workshops on Toning and provides resource tapes and books on Laurel's work.

PO Box 27522, Denver, CO 80228

www.gentlelivingpublications.com
(303) 722-1445